Wellsboro Roots

Memoir of a Civil War Family Legacy

First Edition, September 2014

Library of Congress Cataloging in Publication Data
Sofield Barber, Audrey, 1933-
Wellsboro Roots
p. cm.
ISBN-10:1501050591
ISBN-13:9781501050596

Printed in the United States of America

Wellsboro Roots

Memoir of a Civil War Family Legacy

Audrey Sofield Barber

Dedicated to my cousin, David Finney, without whom this book would not exist. Thank you, David.

TABLE OF CONTENTS

Part Three: Summation

Wellsboro Roots

Memoir of a Civil War Family Legacy

Introduction

This is the first book that I have written. It isn't the first time that I had the desire to write, but it is the first time that I thought that, for the sake of posterity plus my need to grab on to my mysterious past, that this had to be done. I know that there are a lot of people that have more of a clouded history that I have, but most of my history was three thousand miles from where I was born and raised, and to a child, that is on the other side of the Earth.

My dad had been born in Galesburg, Illinois, and somehow ended up in Los Angeles and later in Riverside, California, where he married my mother and I was born. My mom was born in Newark, New Jersey, and when her father left the family they moved to Flint and Detroit, Michigan. I grew up hearing about those last two states like they were paradise. My dad never talked about Illinois as they had moved to Los Angeles when he was just a young man.

My mom was definitely an Eastern type woman…she used to refer to Riverside as a "hick town" with no real culture. As a result, I grew up hearing about the East, how alive people in the East were and how wonderful it was compared to California. A child takes it all in and suddenly she/he thinks it's paradise and so far away that she'll never get to see it, at least, that was my child's eyes take on it.

When my present husband secured employment in Pennsylvania, I thought I was in that Never Never Land. As you read this book you will see the improbable circumstances that brought me to Pennsylvania, and finally Wellsboro, my Never Never Land.

Please don't mistake this for a history book. Nor is it exactly a memoir. A memoir reflects your memory whereas this book is more like a daily log with my thoughts and dreams all wrapped up into one cozy unit. Not being a history book, it won't be complete with references as to where I found different information. My information comes from local history books, Scott Gitchell at the Wellsboro Historical Society, Ancestry.com, et cetera, presented in story form.

Oh, I planted one reference or two now and then, but my study of my ancestral history in Wellsboro is based on what I have found, maybe that day and later to be found out by further investigation that the previous information wasn't quite on track whereby I have to change my story. I don't go back and actually erase what I have put but I just tell what happened as it happened. Hence, it reads as a daily log of discovery.

I have also tried to convey my feelings on my relatives and my impressions of what kind of people they were. Included is much visualization of what it may have been like when my relatives lived in Wellsboro. I even go so far as trying to do my best at psychoanalyzing them. I try to empathize with them—especially my great-grandmother after she was made a widow. What would I have done in this little town if that were me? Was she a strong woman? I say, "Yes. She was." I believe she was a lot stronger and more resourceful than I would have been in her situation and also the situation that many of the ladies of Wellsboro, et cetera, have had to go through.

I look at this adorable little town of Wellsboro with its neatly divided road down Main Street and it glowing gas streetlights and its cleanliness. I then look at the old pictures of what it was like when my ancestors lived here.

They just had dirt and muddy roads, no cars, just horses and buggies. They had drafty houses wood stoves, no air conditioning in the hot summers. There was no inside entertainment like we have today, such as television or computers. They just had each other and in many ways were better off than we are now.

I hope that anybody who reads this book gets as much joy from reading it as I have gotten writing it. I doubt, however, that will happen because when one is writing it, one is living it.

I am eighty-one years old the year this book was published and hope that this book will be passed down to my progeny so that they can get a more clear understanding of from where they came. So come along and do some dreaming of your own while we take a trip down memory lane.

Part One: Discovery

The Beginning of My Genealogy Quest
2004

I think that most people are born with the desire to grab onto their roots. There are some that have no interest in it, but I can remember from the time I was four years old I would crawl up on the couch and say to my mom, "Tell me about when you were little."

Perhaps in a different book, I will go into the history of the Handler (maternal) side of my family; but for now, I will concentrate on my paternal side, the Sofield side. Funny, but I never asked my dad about his history—and for that I feel regret. I think the subject never came up because his parents were still were around. We all lived in Riverside, California, and his parents and brother and sister lived in the greater Los Angeles area and we saw them frequently. This interest in my genealogy all started one day when Brian (my husband) and I were living in Eden, Utah. That was in about 2004. I was just starting to know how to get around on my computer and I visited a free genealogy website and entered all that I knew about my dad's Sofield family. I also included my phone number. Little did I know at the time how simply including my phone number would change the course of my life. It's funny how every little decision that you make can alter your future. Well that specific decision did alter mine because shortly thereafter my phone rang and a man's voice spoke through the other line.

"Is this Audrey Sofield?" he asked.

"Well I used to be," I answered. "But now I am Audrey Barber."

"I am your cousin," he said. "I'm David Finney from Omaha, Nebraska."

And there it was: my first genuine connection. I couldn't have been more thrilled. I remember the moment exactly. I took my phone out on the lawn of the beautiful condominium grounds where we were living and sat and looked at the gorgeous scenery of the valley below and talked and talked with my cousin David.

"Did you know that your great-grandfather, Alfred J. Sofield, was killed at Gettysburg during the Civil War?" That was nearly the first thing that David said to me. It blew me away.

"Was he South or North?" That was my response.

"North," David said.

The lawn in Ogden Valley, Utah, where I first spoke to David.

"Whew," I said.

David told me that his great-great-grandfather was Otis Sofield, who was the youngest brother of my great-grandfather who was the oldest of, I believe, about seven children made up of five boys and two girls. My dad, who was named after his grandfather, was also Alfred J. Sofield. Then David told me that they all came from Wellsboro, Pennsylvania.

After that conversation with David—through which I had learned so much—I ran inside and told Brian. Right away we went to the beautiful Huntsville Library to see what I could find out about the Civil War. We borrowed some videos on the Civil War and came home and watched them.

I am ashamed to say that I had no knowledge of the Civil War at all except that it ended slavery. You have

to realize that I was sixty-nine years old at the time and
when a person is that age and had grown up with little

Wellsboro as it looks today.

knowledge of history, the little things suddenly become
big things. For instance, The Gettysburg Address came to
my mind. That was given only four months after my great-
grandfather, Alfred J. Sofield, was killed: The Gettysburg
Address was written for him!

Think about this: when you are young, you grow
up with the introduction of this great President Abraham
Lincoln and you then have the Gettysburg Address
introduced to you in grade school and you, most likely,
think very little of it—then something happens that
suddenly changes your entire outlook on your family's
place in history. That is exactly what happened to me.

Suddenly I was smitten with learning more about
the Civil War, the Sofield's history and President Lincoln.
Since that time I have read countless books—thick
books—on Lincoln and the War. I did this for the
immediate years that followed.

Then in 2008 I started having some physical problems. I developed breast cancer and had to have one of them removed. A blockage in my heart valve was also discovered and I had to have an angioplasty. Unbelievably, after all that, it was determined that I had a macular hole in my right eye and had to have that taken care of. That left me partially blind in that eye. My health concerns, for obvious reasons, took priority over my genealogy pursuits.

During this same time Brian had taken a job in Uniontown, Pennsylvania. At the conclusion of his work and on his drive home, he stopped by to see his son Lonnie in South Dakota. Lonnie was also in the same land consulting industry.

While visiting Lonnie in South Dakota, the same company for which Lonnie worked hired Brian and he was there for another few months before finally returning to California. He was with me in California for a couple of months and then was rehired and returned to South Dakota. He was only there for about three months: the snow was so bad that they put the job on hold.

Time went on and Brian couldn't find anything else in that industry so we packed up and moved to Maui. We were living on our savings and just as it was about to run out, we got a call from a woman who had worked with him at Uniontown, Pennsylvania. They were hiring Right of Way people in Chambersburg, Pennsylvania. I ran to my computer and loaded MapQuest and entered "Chambersburg." It was only thirty miles from Gettysburg!! I couldn't believe it: Gettysburg!! As it was Brian who was going and not me, I wondered what I was so happy about. Little did I know that this job was the fuel for my still-burning genealogy fire. Long story short, Brian was hired in August of 2011. He and I had a car parked at my daughter Leslie's house in Applegate, California, so that if and when he got work he would fly there, pick up the car and drive to the job. And that is exactly what he did.

I remained on the island of Maui—where Brian loved and he was in Pennsylvania—where I wanted to be. It all seemed a little backward. I stayed on Maui for three months and when he thought that the job looked like it was going to last for a while, he told me to pack up and go see my family in California—and then pack up Leslie and head for Pennsylvania. And that's exactly what *we* did. We flew to Pittsburgh, rented a car and drove to Chambersburg.

Leslie would only be in Pennsylvania for a week so we had to get our Gettysburg fix before she had to head back. We had met a tour guide, Rich Kohr, when Leslie and Kyra, her granddaughter, and I were there briefly in 2008 looking at my great-grandpa's grave.

He was touring someone else and came up to us and wanted to know if we would like him to take our picture over the grave. We accepted. He then said, "I notice that you are looking at Captain Sofield's gravesite, are you related to him?"

A small monument for the 149th Bucktails ...and me.

We told him that we were and he said that he is a
devout follower of the Bucktails and especially the 149th
Pennsylvania Infantry. What were the chances that we
would meet him? Someone who was knowledgeable about
the exact history I was chasing? I took his name and
phone number and kept it safe. Three years later when

Brian told Leslie and me to come to Chambersburg, I called Rich and arranged for a tour of the Sofield trek.

This is where the 149th Company A camped the night before he was killed. That's Leslie and Brian.

He drove us in our rental car and we went to the beautiful battlefield. He first took us to where A.J.'s company camped the day before he was killed. It was a beautiful ranch that was right by a stream. Rich told us that the morning that A.J. was killed, he, being the lead captain of his company, would be the one taking roll call. After they did that, they marched to his death.

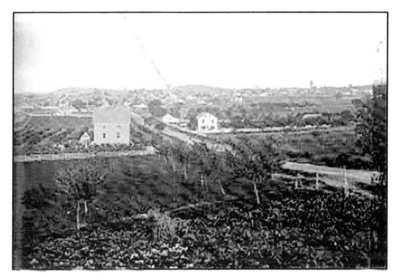

Chambersburg Pike in Gettysburg as it looked in the 1800s.

This is what the barn looks like today.

Rich said that he went to the Civil War Archives in D.C. and saw his signature on the bottom of the roll call *list. It was the last time he signed anything. I never did make it to D.C. that trip, but I sure wanted to go and get a copy of it—which I did in May of 2013.*

Brian's company actually hired me for the three months before his job came to an end. The manager of the company knew that I was into the Civil War and Gettysburg so he assigned me to do some work in the Gettysburg Courthouse. I loved it there. After that job came to an end Brian and I took a trip to Wellsboro and we both loved it right away. Everything is so close to one another, a tight-knit community in every way imaginable.

After a brief stay in Wellsboro, we headed back to Maui and rented an apartment. That lasted for about seven months before Brian was offered a job doing the same land consultation in Bethlehem, Pennsylvania, so away we went and we lived in Stroudsburg in the Poconos for one year and then in December 2013 they assigned him to New Jersey.

We took another trip to Wellsboro during the holidays and fell further in love with the town. After we got back to Stroudsburg, I got to thinking…and I made a proposal to Brian, "Why don't you go ahead to New Jersey and I'll go to Wellsboro and really focus on the research and writing of this memoir? He agreed and said that it would be my project and thought it would be a good idea. (He was probably glad to get rid of me!) So I made a trip to Wellsboro by myself.

All Signs Point to Wellsboro
2004-2013

In my almost daily searches of the Internet since my trip to Gettysburg, I kept leaning more and more about both sides of my family. As for the Sofields I have learned that my grandpa Benjamin Sofield, whom I had known as I was growing up since I was a child, was raised or partially raised in a Veteran's Orphanage. He died when I was about thirteen. He and my grandma, Lillie Belle, lived in El Monte, California, and we would go and see them about once per month.

My grandpa, Benjamin, was kind of a grumpy man. He would sit in his chair in his bedroom with his trusty spittoon next to him and his constantly lit cigar and smoke and spit. He had asthma, thus the spittoon. It was a big brass one and I wish that I had it in my possession. My dad would make me go and sit on his skinny lap. I don't think that my grampa liked kids very much because I would reluctantly pull my skinny legs up to sit on his skinny legs and it wouldn't be long before I got down.

My grandfather had been a blonde with blue eyes in his younger years and he had a huge mustache with little handlebars. He had a round stomach but skinny legs. He hardly talked. He was so different from my grandma, his wife, as she was a typical looking, cute gramma and I would sit happily on her comfortable lap. I remember that she used to use the word "cunning" to mean sweet. If I would recite something for her she would say, "Isn't that cunnin'."

When I think back to what happened to my grandpa when he was young, things that I have learned though my research, I can see why he wasn't the picture of happiness.

When his father went to war he was just a little boy, the baby with two older brothers, namely William and James. A few years ago I sent for my great-grandmother's pension papers and found that it took her ten years to finally get all the money that added up to the $20 per month that she was to receive. She was left with three little boys to care for, and I am not sure if she had any income before that time. In my searches, however, I have found that she had become very entrepreneurial after a few months.

My grandpa, as I mentioned, and one of his older brothers were put in the Mansfield Veterans Orphanage located in the next town. I had been under the impression when I first heard about this that they were put in there for just a little while, but I have found a list of the children that were in there and he was fourteen and his brother was sixteen. Then I found out, when I went to the Wellsboro Historical Society, that the school only kept orphans of military families until they were sixteen. I also saw on that list of kids in that school that one of them was Ella Updyke. My grandmother's maiden name was Updyke and I think that there is some connection there.

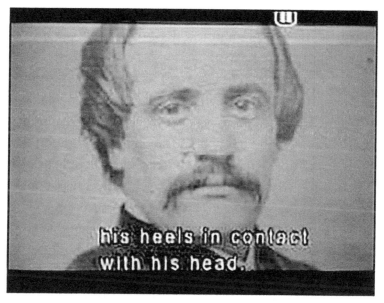

Captain Alfred Sofield

After I did some more investigation I found some old ads in the Wellsboro Agitator (now known as the Wellsboro Gazette). These ads were so telling and made me really appreciate my great-grandmother. I will find and include these ads but for now I will tell you about them.

The ads start by saying that Mrs. A.J. Sofield has just returned from a trip to New York with new millinery goods that she is selling. That wasn't so impressive in and of itself until I saw that there were more ads that were stating that she had just returned with a new batch of goods…these were about every two weeks. I have taken three trips to Wellsboro and have found the approximate place where she lived and have seen pictures of what that little sleepy town looked like in the 1800s. They, of course, had dirt roads, et cetera.

My great-grandfather, her husband, had been the Justice of the Peace. From what I have been able to conclude, they lived right next door or so from the courthouse where he worked.

Anyway, I am not sure at this point what portion of New York she had to go travel to get this material but I do figure that she had to take a horse and buggy from her place (maybe with her children if their grandmother, Julia Sofield, did not watch them for her) either directly to New York or to the train depot from which she perhaps took a train. Then she would get back on her horse and buggy and return back to Wellsboro. Anyway, the fact that she did it was very brave of her. Along with this ambition, she was probably heartbroken—being a widow.

I have made three trips to Wellsboro and have picked up a little information on each visit. The first time we went there was in May of 2011 right after our job in Chambersburg and Gettysburg came to an end.

The minute we pulled up to the little divided street called Main Street, Brian and I were *so* impressed. We stayed two nights in the Penn Wells Hotel that has been there since the late 1800s. We went to the movie theatre, which was right next door, and saw *The Three Stooges*. We took walks up and down the cute little town that reminded me of the 1950's.

There isn't a mall closer than one hour away.
There have been attempts at it but the town fathers want
it to stay just the way it is and I hope that they always
succeed. There are old churches on many corners that are
architecturally idyllic.

While we were in Wellsboro, I went to the Tioga
County Recorders Office (Wellsboro is the county seat)
and pulled some deeds that were from A.J. Sofield. One
deed revealed that he took the oath of office when he
became the Justice of the Peace. Then there were real
estate transactions showing that he bought properties.
Some looked like investment properties and the other two
were where his house and a small orchard were, and from
what I can decipher, they are contiguous to each other and
are very close to the court house.

*This is the courthouse where A.J. Sofield was Justice of the Peace. In
older pictures, there were no pillars, just steps.*

In 2013 when Brian and I moved to Stroudsburg,
Pennsylvania, we went on another little 168-mile trip to

Wellsboro and stayed in a beautiful little Bed & Breakfast at 3 Charles Street called "Inn on the Green." While there I went back to the County Recorder's Office and had to re-pull some documents as we had the others left in Hawaii in storage.

This time I looked them over more carefully and found that a document regarding the place right next door to the courthouse where they lived gave some descriptions that I hadn't noticed before. The properties were between Main Street and Water Street and backed up to a hill.

I walked over there and started walking off the feet and it became somewhat more apparent where the location was. The problem that I was—and am—having is that in the description the properties are contiguous of other properties from east to west by just naming the owners of record of that time. That didn't help me much.

* * *

There is a book on the Civil War called *The 149th Pennsylvania Volunteer Infantry Unit in the Civil War.* That book tells all about the Wellsboro men that were involved in answering the call from President Lincoln to volunteer for the army. My great-grandfather was mentioned quite a few times in the first four chapters of the book. Anyone interested in the Bucktails and their daily movements from day one of their recruitment until the end of the war in 1865, should read this book.

On page eight in the first chapter, the author states: "In the Northern Tier counties of Tioga and Potter, war meetings were held in early August to provide a bounty for volunteers to meet Lincoln's call for troops.

The August 6, 1862 issue of the Wellsboro, Tioga column cautioned volunteers for the nine month regiments that recruits would no longer be accepted after August 19th, and that if the quota was not filled soon, "the Governor will have to resort to drafting" "Alfred J. Sofield, (which was my Dad's name also, my brackets) a 32 year old Wellsboro Justice of the Peace and former Clerk to the Board of Commissioners (the same commissioners that held the war meetings encouraging volunteering), began recruiting men for a Bucktail Company."

It goes on to tell how they marched to the train station that would take them to Harrisburg and to a camp called Camp Curtin. Andrew Curtin was the governor at the time and they were under the command of Colonel Roy Stone. Once they arrived at Camp Curtin. Another paragraph gives me pride mixed with sorrow. It says: "Discipline had to come before entering the gates of Camp Curtin. These were the company officers who were identified as such while recruiting the company in the home county. Some had previous military experience...but most were made officers because of their recruiting ability. Usually they were popular people in the community: the local lawyer, politician, blacksmith, general store proprietor, postmaster or tavern keeper, men that made friends and were friends due to their occupations. They were expected to bring some order to camp life." I was *so* proud that my great-grandfather was compared to the local tavern keeper.

After staying in Camp Curtain and at the end of August 1862, they were ordered to go to D.C. The Confederates were trying very hard to either kidnap or kill President Lincoln so they were to go there to protect him.

It reads: "After getting off the train they marched up Pennsylvania Avenue through deep mud, the men, not accustomed to the weight of their field equipment, dragged the column into a slow march." Moving north on 14th Street, they were so tired that they lay down on the damp lawns and slept. Their destination was Meridian Hill, located a mile northeast of Kalorama Heights.

In another place in this book it states that from Meridian Hill "the men could look out over the city and watch the activity. It goes on to quote another relative named Wallace Sofield who said, "Our Company is detailed to guard the Carver Hospital. We have to stand guard four hours in every twenty-four. We are camped about two miles from the city in a nice hardwood grove which is called Meridian Hill. We could hear heavy firing on Tuesday (Sept. 2nd) at Bull Run and Manassas Junction. All of our army is here and about Washington. They say that Old Abe has given orders for us to march to Bull Run, but that ain't so."

In 2008 my daughter, Leslie, and her granddaughter, Kyra and I took a trip to Springfield, Illinois, stayed with friends, saw many Lincoln artifacts such as his home before he was president and his burial site. Then we went to New York and D.C. While in D.C. we tried hard to find this Meridian Hill but we were mainly on foot and couldn't find it. We now have the address—23rd and S Street in D.C.—and I'll probably never be there again. *Darn!*

Meridian Hill, according to Wikipedia, was a lookout for the soldiers to see if the Confederates were coming. I guess you could see quite a bit from that hill. Also that whole area was and still is a very upper class area with beautiful homes….not a lookout for men wielding guns.

Kalorama Heights.

"Regarding the 149th Pennsylvania Infantry commanded by Lieutenant Colonel Walton Dwight, the unit, part of the 2nd Brigade of the Third Division of the I Corps, arrived on the field by traversing Emmitsburg Road, and deploying north and west of the McPherson farm house west of the town of Gettysburg, linking with the 150th Pennsylvania on their left and the 143rd Pennsylvania on their right.

Dedicated in November 1888, this monument marks the area where the 149th Pennsylvania Infantry "Bucktails" were positioned through its most intense fighting on the First Day of the Battle of Gettysburg (July 1, 1863).

Here they received a great barrage of artillery from Confederates on Herr Ridge, which caused them a number of casualties (Captain Alfred J. Sofield of Company A was split in half and killed by a shot that also killed two other men), which prompted Lieutenant Colonel Dwight to move the regiment's colors fifty yards north of the unit. The move effectively fooled the Confederates for a time and drew their fire away from the main body. When the Confederate infantry attacked from Oak Hill, they were repulsed several times by the 149th Pennsylvania, who even affected two successful charges past the unfinished Railroad Cut north of them. However, the increasing pressure put on them by the numerically superior Confederates caused the Union lines to collapse, and the 149th Pennsylvania's position became outflanked and untenable.

With the regiment's colors still far in front of them, Colonel Dwight ordered a retreat, rather than try to recover the flags, knowing that such an attempt would destroy his regiment. (He wrote in his after-battle report "I lost the colors but saved the regiment.")

He had been severely wounded in the leg while a portion of his unit was in the Railroad Cut, and for a time, the unit had no effective field officers due to their all having been either killed or confused during retreat. The regiment's Company D, which had been detached to this point as the provost guard for the 1st Division, arrived on the field, and put up a heroic twenty minute stand near the Shultz House on Chambersburg Pike, which gave retreating troops more time to get away.

Company D's Captain James Glenn took command of the survivors upon finding out of that he was the only unwounded officer of the regiment, and led those he could find through the town to Cemetery Hill south of Gettysburg. Like many Union units that day, they lost a number of men captured when victorious Confederates overwhelmed the town itself.

This is now a parking lot for the little R.E.Lee Headquarters and also a motel behind it.

By the end of July 1 the remnants who were stationed with the Union left, but were soon moved to the center, where on the Third day they helped support the repulse of Pickett's Charge (a third monument for the unit was placed in this area). The regiment came to Gettysburg with 460 effective men. It lost 66 killed or mortally wounded (including Color Sergeant Henry Brehm, who was mortally wounded trying to save the regiment's colors), 159 wounded, and 111 missing or captured, for a total of 336 out of the 460." (Russ Dodge)

I took the above photograph in front of Robert E. Lee's headquarters which is still here as a museum. If you follow the street right down to where the slope just starts its upward swing, Captain Sofield was caught and killed in the crossfire. (The little town of Gettysburg is behind us.)

You can see the treed ridge behind the barn and that is where the cannons were fired from. It's called Herr's Ridge to this day.

After they camped all night, they got up and marched towards the town of Gettysburg. They had to cross a covered bridge called Sach's Bridge and it is also still here to this day.

Sach's Bridge

Welcome to Wellsboro
December 2, 2013

On December 2, 2013, I, at 80 years young, took off by myself and headed to Wellsboro to spend two days and nights looking for a rental.

The homes in Wellsboro are all old and beautifully kept and upgraded from the 1800s. Most of them are Victorian style. It makes you feel so good just walking down the street, no malls, no Wal-Mart's, pleasant and happy faces everywhere. Everyone knows each other.

I bought a newspaper and started calling landlords and looking for places. The rents here are relatively inexpensive. In Stroudsburg, we pay $1303 each month— and in New Jersey it's even higher. Our Stroudsburg place is furnished but it's still expensive compared to Wellsboro.

I looked at a couple of places and they were just too big for only me, even though they were only $700 per month. After I came back to the Bed and Breakfast I went to my room and it had one of those little fireplaces with fake fire but it wasn't putting out any warmth. I called the office and the next thing I knew there was a knock on my bedroom door and there was a lady that introduced herself as Nelle. It turned out that she owned two Bed and Breakfasts. This one and another one two doors over. She came in and we started talking. I told her why I was there and, in brief, she said that she really liked and trusted me and she wanted to know if I would be interested in renting the whole house from her.

The Packer House at 133 Main Street.

It came with all the furniture, washer/dryer, dishwasher/disposal and get this: maid service. Yes, the maid will come in twice per month and change the sheets and give me fresh towels, all for an affordable rent per month including utilities.

She told me to think it over. Two seconds later, after fainting and returning to consciousness, I said that I had thought it over and let's shake hands. Actually, we hugged. She also invited me to come next door the next morning and the morning after that for a wonderful homemade breakfast by Amanda, the sweet little Mennonite cook.

This is Amanda

Amanda wears the little white cap and a long dress. She has the most wonderful personality: always laughing and, it seems, always happy. She is only twenty-five years old and has three jobs. She lives with her parents and brothers. Her parents are farmers who grow vegetables year round in green houses. Pennsylvania has many Mennonite and Amish folks that grow year round. That would sure help sustain one in Pennsylvania winters.

Then I met the couple that was staying upstairs for two nights, Hunter and Lucy. They were from Australia and were traveling around the world. We stayed up late that night laughing while I made fun of the way they talked. I made more friends there in one day than I had made in Stroudsburg in eleven months.

I did some more research and went to get some more documents and found that my great-grandfather and his brother, John, had done a real estate transaction with a Dr. Nathan Packer. I pulled the deed, not thinking much of it, and when I got back to the B&B there was a picture in the living room of the house as it looked in the 1840s. It had been built by Dr. Nathan Packer. He lived in it in the 1840's.

I couldn't believe it, that I was probably staying in a house that, maybe, my relatives had been in.

There is a beautiful old mansion—that is now the library—right across the street from the house where I am staying. I went over there and searched through a book and found Dr. Packer's picture and another picture of the house as it looked back then.

If you look up the house on Google.com, you can see it. It's called the "Packer House of Wellsboro, PA." I will get the entire place to myself starting the 28th of December until 28th of May.

Looking through the window from where I type at the library across the street.

The library.

Winter Wonderland
December 31, 2014

Well, here we are, our second day here in
Wellsboro. I finally unpacked and separated the things
that Brian has to take back to New Jersey with him and set
myself up here in
My Winter Wonderland.

I went to the grocery store and bought some more
groceries so that I could cook a cozy dinner tonight. You
are going to hear the word *cozy* a lot in this book, as *cozy* is
common amongst the females in my family.

After that little shopping event I came back,
unloaded and since it was New Years Eve day I knew that
if I was going to go to any of the federal buildings for
information that I had better get to it. The next thing I
did was walk out the door to the sidewalk, turned right
and walked past two houses to the corner, crossed the

street, turned right, crossed the street and went past a church and to the Wellsboro Historical Society.

The man in there, Scott Gitchell, knows me now as I have gone there each time I was in town. He is an expert on local history so I love talking to him. When I told him that I suspected that I knew where my great-grandparents had lived he didn't think that I was right because it was a

Scott knows everybody in Wellsboro....and speaks of the people who lived here in the 1800s like they're buddies. He runs the local Historical Society.

commercial area and it had been all these years. He said that it was on the same street but up the street more in the opposite direction. He told me to bring my deeds in to his office next week and we'd go over them. Wow, if that's the case, that makes it closer to where I am living right now…maybe just across the street and over a couple of doors.

Then I went next door to the Court House in the recorder's office and asked them a couple of questions and they gave me a couple of answers. Then when I walked out of the building, there was Brian across the street taking a walk to town (another block down). To those of you who don't understand *cozy*…that was cozy!

I then came home and cooked dinner, ate in the cozy dining area and got on the computer. Then my phone rang: it was the landlady's granddaughter (the massage therapist) making an appointment for my massage next Tuesday.

Everything will be closed tomorrow, but my search will still continue.

Celia

January 3, 2014

As you recall, in one of my previous chapters I
mentioned that when I first made that trip alone here to
Wellsboro to find a rental, I had talked to landlords—
Celia being one of them—on the phone that had an
apartment for rent. Then soon after I had spoken with her
I found this beautiful B&B that I was going to get for a
nominal rental amount and we shook hands (hugged) on
it. I think in Wellsboro a hug is an agreement.

Then, I had to call Celia and tell her that I had
gotten this place and we spoke for a while and hung up.
Then she called me back and asked me to have lunch with
her when I moved here. Well, that luncheon was done
today and it was a delight. What was so amazing to me is
that she looked like she belonged in my mother's family;
she even looked a little like me. She is one year younger
than I am and thinks a lot like I do about world affairs.

Celia and I also discovered that we both have Jewish in us, she, being Russian Jew and I being Austrian Jew. I actually had my DNA done and I am almost ½ on my mother's side, whose parents were born and raised in Austria and Alsace, France. I did a little looking into that and found that when my Handler Grandmother was born, Austria controlled Alsace Lorraine. (That was just a little sidebar for you).

Celia told me that her husband is writing a book that is also based on the history of his family here in Wellsboro. I really am so surprised at how much this little burg is buried in its history. It's like those people of the past are still here with us…and in a way, we are keeping them alive through our research and reporting.

I also found something out from Celia that made me feel good. I had it in my mind that my poor great-grandmother, Helen Sofield, had to ride a horse and buggy a long way to the train station to get to New York for her millinery goods every week, and then come back the same way, but that is not necessarily so. Celia said that there is/was a train station right here in town. I have yet to go and check on it but I will.

We had lunch at Harland's Family Restaurant on Pearl Street, just one block behind Main Street and two blocks from my house. I had to park a block away and trudge through the snow for a whole block, watching every step to make sure that I didn't fall and break my hip. That's all I'd need and it would all be over. It was so pretty because the snow is about a foot deep and, to me, it's beautiful. I took a picture of the street with my phone and sent it to my daughter Leslie and she wrote back, "Here it's like Spring and I hate it. Yesterday at the Mall I saw people in shorts and flip flops." That was in Auburn and Roseville, California. The girls in my family love winter and the boys love the outdoor weather.

Celia told me that she belongs to a ladies club that is, naturally, right across the street from me and held twice per month and she invited me to go and join. Then she told me about an art show that is going to be held next week and it is, you guessed it, right across the street from me.

Everything is right across the street from me. My gasoline bill is going to go down, down, down; I know my car insurance did. When I go to those events I will get to meet more people and hopefully my business cards will be here by then. Celia said that what they do at this club is decide on a subject and write about it and then the next week everyone reads what they have written. I asked her what she had written about and she said Eleanor Roosevelt. Co-incidentally, I bought a biography of Mrs. Roosevelt a few years ago and she was a wonderful person. Celia and I discussed that for a few minutes. I am anxious to go to the meeting next week and hear what she wrote.

I'm All Alone Now

January 4, 2014

Brian helped me pack and moved me up here to Wellsboro from Stroudsburg, Pennsylvania, where we had been living. The plan was for him to go back in a couple of days but while he was here he got a bad head cold. The flu is now hitting hard in twenty-five states, including Pennsylvania so we didn't want to take any chances.

Brian and I decided that he would leave today, because the weather is clear and the next two days will be rainy with thunder and lightning: not good for traveling. This big, beautiful house that I am in is large and lonely with him gone. We are usually together every day all day, so I will be writing today in the living room with a heavy heart.

The Formal Living Room

A while ago I had to go to the post office and I am not used to driving in snow and ice, but I chanced going that treacherous six blocks. I put the car in four-wheel drive and braved it on down. My windshield was encrusted in ice and as soon as I scraped it off, it seemed to come back. By the time I had gotten to the post office it had somewhat iced over again. I got out of the car and walked to the curb where the mailboxes were and when I turned to come back to the car there was a man scraping my windshield.

Wow. I didn't know if I was supposed to pay him, like you do in Tijuana when the young boys come up and start cleaning your windows or what. I kind of gave him the once over to see if he looked like he needed a dollar or something but he was just dressed like a regular resident.

I asked him if he did this for a living or if he just happened by and saw a lady in distress. He said, "I was just sitting there in my car waiting for my wife to come out of the post office and I could see that your car wasn't road ready for snow."

That little deed lifted my lonely spirits for a time. Just being reminded of what a friendly little town this is helped. I'm starting to feel like part of it, like I belong. I'm very anxious to go to some of those little meetings, et cetera, that I've been invited to and meet more of these nice people.

As I look out this window that is in front of my computer desk, I can't help but visualize seeing my great-grandfather walking to work. The courthouse is across the street to my right and we figured, so far, that his house was across the street a little to my left. So there he is, walking a fast pace in his long black coat and wool, knitted cap on his head to keep his ears warm. Right now the sun is out and shining little silver sparkles in the snow. It's so utterly beautiful. I wonder what his hat looked like? Could it have been like this one?

Or maybe this sporty one?

After all he was Justice of the Peace so maybe this one with ear muffs.

Just sayin.'

Part Two: Research

Treasure Trove Sunday
January 5, 2014

I woke up today feeling pretty good. I had planned on going to the Presbyterian Church with my friend, Celia, but she wasn't feeling up to it. The reason that I was going was to meet that attorney who knows a lot about the history of Wellsboro. I bundled up and walked over to it (across the street, of course) and took a picture of the front of it, the inside and stood on the steps and took a picture of my house, which is right across the street (of course) from the steps of the church.

I spoke with a lady inside for a moment and then decided that I should be going to the Episcopalian Church which is the one that my great-grandparents were members of and was located one block behind and one block over from my house. So I walked over to that church and got there early.

That church and all the churches here are architecturally beautiful. As I was early, I went inside to a little waiting room. I then went into the main hall: it was quite lovely. I kept staring at the ceiling that was so awe striking. There were huge open beams that went in all sorts of directions. After a while the minister, or priest, as he is called, came in wearing a long robe. As the services began I counted the parishioners there. Including the choir and myself and there were thirty.

During the service there was an altar boy about sixteen years old and another older man that assisted the Rector...all wearing the long robes. I began to see the semblance of the Catholic Church. There was a kneeling board under the pew in front of me like the Catholic Churches have but only two parishioners were using it.

There weren't as many rituals that the Catholics have, but there were some. The Rector gave a short and friendly sermon and then there was some singing. One nice thing that I enjoyed was there was a little one minute break where we all got up and shook hands with others saying, "peace." Everyone was smiling.

After the service was over, about an hour in total, we all walked back to a big area with round tables and chairs. They had some goodies to eat along with coffee. There were three other ladies at that table and then the Rector came and joined us. It was at that table that I got some good news.

When I told them why I was in Wellsboro, they all came up with stories and ideas. But there was one lady that really got my attention. I had told them that the reason that I came to that church service was because my great-grandparents had belonged to it and I wanted to be as familiar as I could with how they thought. I was really surprised to see the Catholic leanings of this religion because no one in my family that I knew of ever went to the Catholic Church….now that I think of it they didn't go to any church.

I asked the Rector if he knew where the old Episcopal Church was in the 1800s and he said, "right across the street, but it's gone and there is a house there now." One of the ladies, Joan Hart, told me that she had one of the chairs that came out of that old church. Wow. My family may have sat on it, who knows.

Then I asked the Rector if he had any archives with a list of the parishioners that go back to the 1800s and he said that he does and for me to call him tomorrow and he'd let me go over there and go through them. That will, of course, be some of what I will be doing tomorrow.

After that I came home and did some more research and remembered that there was going to be an art showing at 2PM. Yes, it was to be "right across the street." (I'm not lying about this, everything is "right across the street.") My car is going to get very lonely.

I went to the art showing and met a lot of people. Everyone wanted me to go here and there for information. These people are all so proud of their little town and the townspeople. It reminds me so much of a movie. I'm still waiting for the other shoe to drop…but hope it won't.

Civil War Round Table Invitation
January 6, 2014

I am having a hard time remembering all the referral contacts that people have been giving me. They all want to help. One in particular turned out rather interesting. I was told to call a certain person, and at this time, I don't remember his name. Tsk Tsk. Remember, I'm 80!!

Anyway, I called this man because he was a Civil War enthusiast and may have come across the Sofield name. While talking to him for a time he told me of a Civil War Round Table meeting that they have, I believe, once per month in the next town over, Mansfield. He invited me to go but I told him that being a Californian I wasn't used to driving in the snow and ice. He then offered to pick me up and take me. Soooo I have a date tomorrow night! The first thing that I asked him was, "Are you a safe driver?" Gee, I wonder what he was going to say...would it be, "No?" That is a silly question to ask anyone but I think that it makes one feel safer if they ask, it keeps them on their toes.

Today the ice wasn't as prevalent as it was yesterday and we'll see what Wednesday brings, as that is when I go to the Civil War Round Table.

I also hired a very nice young man to help me with my computer. He works at the high school as a computer tech for the classes and the administration. His name is Shane Cleveland and so very adept at what he does. He was here at my house for 1 ½ hours and did a very good job. He put my new printer together for me and showed me some short cuts. I wonder if I am going to meet anyone over here that I am *not* impressed with. Not so far, anyway.

Tomorrow I am going to treat myself to a massage with hot rocks. I can't wait. Even though doing this is fun, I am trying to keep up my pace and there is some stress involved. How's that for rationalizing?

Nelle, Lori, Laura Lee and Amanda
January 7, 2014

If I have anyone to be appreciative of and thankful for their true loving spirits, it's the people in this chapter title. Nelle is the sweet lady that so graciously let me live in this beautiful Victorian type home for so little. Her personality is so upbeat, always smiling and hugging.

Lori is her daughter and she is so upbeat and such a fun person...a person that if anyone was sad, they wouldn't be sad for long after being in her company for a short period of time. She is here for a short time and is going to back Dallas, Texas, for some surgery and then she'll be back. I just hope that I am still her she returns.

Then there is Laura Lee. She is the granddaughter of Nelle, married and the mother of a daughter. Laura Lee has her own spa business. She is just precious. Her eyes actually sparkle when she talks. She gave me a full massage yesterday (January 7th) for an hour and a half. I

could just feel the relaxing difference this morning when I woke up. My right
hip usually is in pain, but so far, so good.

I had previously mentioned Amanda, the young Mennonite girl who does all the cooking and bookkeeping for the B&Bs in a previous chapter but I just can't say enough about her. Just her voice is enough to make one

Amanda, Nelle and Lori

smile. If she were ever sad, you wouldn't know it as she seems happy all the time. I see her out shoveling snow, light snow, of course, but never a complaint, always a smile. She's the picture of innocence. I have a feeling that her parents are very proud of her.

Does this sound like a movie, a movie that seems to make me sound like a Pollyanna of sorts? I just know that I am not exaggerating, at least so far. If it's a dream I don't want to wake up.

As a postscript to this seemingly fictional story, the maid is coming in today to do some cleaning. No no no no, this isn't happening, but…please…DON'T pinch me.

Another Treasure Trove
January 8, 2014

Well today was going to be a busy day. Regardless of the freezing temperature, I just had to get over to the Episcopal Church and see those archives. Prior to my departure there was a flurry of ladies cleaning this house (wow) and then the TV man was coming to upgrade the cable and fix their computer that they keep here for bookkeeping.

Then my glasses had come apart and I had to go and pick them up…all the while trying to keep a window of opportunity open to get to those archives. So I thought, I'll just walk, yes, that's right, across the street (this time it was the side street, but still just across the street) to the eye doctor's office and after I picked them up I decided to just walk another block to the church and take a quick look at those archives.

Well, the Priest (he prefers to be called Father Hinton, so, Father Hinton) was there and he had three books, each one with a date on it. One was 1830s and up, the others were 1870s and up and then there was one that was 1900s. I picked up the 1830s one and he said, "Here let me show you how to use the books."

He opened it up to page 100. And there it was, right there on the top left hand page: "Helen Sofield baptized on October 13, 1858." Of course I yelled and he jumped. I said, "That's my great grandmother right there!!!!"

Oh, my gosh, on the very page that he opened, there she was. It's almost like I am being led around to find these things. I feel that that isn't true but something is making this easy, not to mention thrilling.

The priest left the room, holding his ears (kidding), and I started turning pages and there back a few pages were my great-great-grandparents' baptisms and two of their other children. Now Helen was their daughter-in-law, but I didn't see Alfred in there. I'm not surprised: I have a feeling that he was too wrapped up in business and secular things to care much about religion...but I may be wrong.

January 8, 2014, PM

I was getting really anxious to go to this Round Table gathering and at 6:PM sharp, Roger Wagner was here to pick me up. He was a very nice gentleman and he told me that he and his wife presently worship at the Presbyterian Church that I can see looking out my window. The reason that he was interested in the Civil War was because of a trilogy of books he had read that were written by Bruce Catton to celebrate the 100th anniversary of our nation's Civil War.

To some, it may be hard to understand why so many people are fascinated with that war, but on thinking of it further, it does make sense. If you picture that you may be living in, maybe, Ohio or New York, et cetera, and you have relatives that you have been close to all your lives and suddenly you're faced with more than the belligerent Uncle John, who lives in South Carolina who always come to the Christmas dinner at your house each year, that you merely disagree with, you are now facing the fact that you may have to assist in his death.

Other countries go through this often and we read about it, and then go on to the funny papers, but when it's in your own back yard, it takes on a life of its own. I remember a year and a half ago when I worked in Gettysburg, a really cute and quiet little burg, I used to think about those poor people suddenly looking out in their back yards and seeing men with guns killing each other. It's no wonder that we are awestruck by this war: it was a personal war. It seems that I digressed a bit. So on with the meeting.

When we drove the ten or so miles to Mansfield, I noticed the difference between that town and Wellsboro. The Mansfield people, as I found out, are just as in love with their town as the Wellsboro people are but the difference in the layout of the town itself is what's most different: it's more spread out. As we approached the town (it was dark outside) you could see the lights of its layout that looked like it was pretty big but Mr. Wagner told me that the population over there was less than Wellsboro. Wellsboro is simply more condensed.

Mr. Wagner and I walked into the meeting and it was a large room with tables and a kitchen with goodies there to tempt me. I found out later that it was part of a church. There were three other ladies there and the rest were men. I was glad to see that there were ladies there, too.

The moderator was Dr. Bob Wooley, whose doctorate was in history. He is a very easy person to listen to, very amiable. I was given to understand that on each of these monthly meetings they usually consist of Dr. Wooley emailing people an article on something about the Civil War and then having a discussion about it the next meeting. This time, though, he showed a movie called *Pharoahs Army*, which was a movie about an event that was supposed to have really happened. It was an interesting movie and we had a discussion about it afterwards. I really enjoyed it and am looking forward to going next month.

After the meeting closed I went up to Dr. Wooley and told him that my grandpa and his brother had been more or less raised in the Veterans Orphanage in this town after his dad had been killed in Gettysburg.

The orphanage my grandfather attended.

He was just a young boy when his dad was killed but the children had to be at least five before they could go there...so maybe my great-grandmother had to wait a couple of years before she sent him there.

I asked Dr. Wooley if he knew of this school and he told me right where to find where it used to be and that it's been razed since the early 1900s but there is a plaque on the property dedicated to it. It was a very enjoyable evening and I look forward to it for next month.

The plaque that you see on the previous page is in front of the Veteran's Orphanage where my grampa and his brother James had to go when their dad was killed. For instance, I found out from the local Historical Society that in that school you had be at least five years old to be admitted and you couldn't stay longer than when you either turned sixteen or if you were allowed to finish out the year after you turned sixteen. Then I go to Ancestry.com for the following information and I find that record show him to be eighteen. I will have to go to the Historical Society and see what Scott Gitchell says about this.

This from the 1870 United States Federal Census regarding Benjamin Sofield and other residents of the orphanage: Do any of you recognize any last names here?

Name:	Benjamin Sofield
Age in 1870:	18
Birth Year:	abt 1852
Birthplace:	Pennsylvania
Home in 1870:	Mansfield, Tioga, Pennsylvania
Race:	White
Gender:	Male
Post Office:	Tioga
Value of real estate:	View Image

	Name	Age
Household Members:	Phebe Fling	15
	Eliza Fling	13
	Eliza Godden	17
	Hiram Grames	13

Melvin Grames	11
George Gilmore	14
Thomas Hotchkiss	13
Sarah Hand	14
James Hand	11
Lucy Hulslander	14
Clarissa Hulslander	12
Sarra Hall	14
Selina King	15
John King	11
James Kibbe	14
Amara Darley	14
Hannah Lover	14
Lucinda Labar	15
Henrietta Labar	14
Mary Martin	15
George Martin	9
James Mathew	12
John Mathew	12
Leisi Mccann	15
Elisha Newton	12
Louisa Hall	14
Adaline Newton	15
Rachel Olden	17
Lydia Olden	12
Carrie Pepperman	12
Elsie Pepperman	14
Alice Pince	14
Charles Pett	14
John Pett	14
Isabella Rogus	9
Emma Ribble	14

Henry Saxton	13
Millard Saxton	14
Eli Simmons	13
Eunice Simmons	16
Orion Smith	11
Horace Smith	17
Ellen Smith	10
Cora Smith	11
Helen B Smith	10
James Sofield	15
Benjamin Sofield	18
James Snyder	14
Eugene Saxbury	18
Harland Saxbury	10
Edward Shepherd	12
Ellen Shepherd	8
Delmina Shepherd	7
George Tolulay	13
Clewellyn Updyke	10
Ella Updyke	15
Archie Vamingen	15
Levi Vamingen	14
Agnes Vamingen	11
Clarissa Vamingen	8
Van Mary Herren	15
Charles Herren	12
Ellen Welch	13
Mary Watts	10
Abbie Welch	14
Merton White	14
John Watts	14
James Watts	12

Frank Wilcox	15
Wesley Wilcox	12
Daniel Wilcox	13
Wellington Wheeland	14
Harriet Ward	15
Juleette Ward	13
Willis Westbrook	12
Edward Westbrook	10
Charles Blackman	14
Irvin Butter	11
Ada Butter	9
Daniel Bockus	10
Stella Wade	22
Mary Wade	43
Augusta Owens	32

Sofield,
12- James
1878 Sept. D M.

Died—Mrs. A.J. Sofield (reports) that her son, James M. Sofield, died on Friday. The dec'd was 23 years of age and was the 2nd son of the late Capt. Alfred J. Sofield, who was killed at Gettysburg. The funeral was held at the residence of his mother on Main Street.

In memoriam—the following resolutions were unammously adopted at a meeting of Alert Hose Company held Friday, Sept. 13th, 1878: Whereas, It has pleased Almighty God to

remove from our midst our
brother fireman, James M.
Sofield, be it Resolved, that
his sudden death we lose a
kind hearted brother, and a
good fireman - - -that we
tender to his bereaved Mother
and brothers our sincere
sympathy.

James, two years older than my grandfather, had
also attended the Veteran's Orphanage.

The Agitator
January 9, 2014

In all my years, and there are plenty, and as far as I
know, my Aunt Helen from La Puente, California, was the
only family member involved in politics. I remember I
would go and stay there for a week at a time when I was
about 10-13. They were money people. They had a large
farm and behind the hedge that was protecting them from
the workers that stayed in the little cottage in the back,
there were acres and acres of vegetables growing. They
also raised racehorses and they would take me to the races
that their horses would be running in.

I remember one time that Aunt Helen (obviously
named after my great-grandmother) took me to former
President Nixon's home (at a time prior to his presidency).
He wasn't there but his wife was. I had remembered that
Nixon must have been running for political office when

my Aunt Helen and I went to their home. I believe that my Aunt was campaigning for him but not sure. I just remember going to their house for a short visit. He lived in San Clemente and she lived in La Puente about 55 miles away.

As my Aunt Helen and Mrs. Nixon talked I remember looking at how fancy their home was. So stepping back to that time, I can see that she was probably the only one in my family to inherit my great-granddad's love of politics. Had he lived, he may have been more of a familiar figure in his time. The article on the next page, taken from *The Agitator*, dated August 1859, it was just two years before the Civil War started and four years before it took all those aspirations away from him. He is referred to in this—and most—article as A.J. Sofield.

Looking back at my Dad's newspaper write-ups you also see A.J. Sofield, not for political news clips, but for entertainment. He was a violinist and grew up as a self-taught student, like his mother, my Gramma Lilly Belle, only hers was piano.

Please read this article. Had he lived, who knows…

THE TIOGA COU

Republican County Convention.

From our own Reporter.

TIOGA, August 26, 1859

From ten o'clock in the morning till one o'clock in the afternoon the streets about the different hotels presented a lively appearance. Candidates for the different nominations were eagerly canvassing the delegates,—politicians were presenting their "claims",—delegates were "button-holed," especially those who were not instructed,—figuring was going on till every rule known in politics was tested,—when the bell rang for the assembling of the Delegates in one of the school rooms. The room was large enough to accommodate the delegates and all of the spectators who chose to come in.

The Convention was called to order by S. B. Beeman, Esq. T. L. BALDWIN was chosen President, and A. J. SOFIELD and I. M. BODINE were chosen Secretaries. The President then announced the Convention organized.

The delegates were then called from the different Townships and Boroughs—sixty-six in all. They are as follows:

Bloss.—John James, I. M. Bodine.
Brookfield.—C. E. Phillips, J. E. Mintonye.
Charleston.—A. E. Niles, John Francis.
Covington Boro.—J. L. Miller, G. W. Kelts.
" *Tsp.*—S. F. Richards, R. S. Marvin.
Chatham.—Owen Allen, R. Toles.
Clymer.—A. A. Amsbry, Henry Steele.
Delmar.—H. S. Hastings, Wm. English.
Deerfield.—H. E. Potter, Newton Bulkley.
Elk.—J. F. Westcott, Jebial Beach.
Elkland.—Leander Culver, Stewart Dailey.

Farmington.—John Vandusen, Jas. Beebe.
Gaines.—B. V. Ogden, D. K. Marsh.
Jackson.—Chas. Voorhes, Edgar Kriner.
Lawrence.—M. S Baldwin, Dyer Power.
Lawrenceville —J. C. Beeman, Royal Wheeler.
Liberty.—G. R. Sheffer, G. W. Childs.
Knoxville.—Wm. Tiffany, J. H. Stubbs.
Mainsburg.—E. A. Fish, D. S. Peters.
Mansfield.—Mart King, A. J. Ross.
Middlebury.—O. M Stebbins, O P. McClure.
Morris.—Enoch Blackwell, W. W. Babb.
Nelson.—T. R. Warren, Perry Daily.
Osceola —Russell Crandall, John Tubbs.
Rutland.—I. S. Horton, A. G. Argotsinger.
Richmond.—D. C. Holden, Jas. M. Rose.
Shippen.—E. Seagers, John Dickinson.
Sullivan.—L. Gray, L. G. Bradford.
Tioga —T. L. Baldwin, H. S. Johnson.
Union.—John Irvin. Anson Dann.
Ward.—Andrew Kniffin, Abram Kniffin.
Wellsboro.—A. J Sofield, P. C Hoig.
Westfield.—Charlton Phillips, E. G. Hill.

The Chairman and Secretaries acted as a Committee on credentials.

The President stated that the first business in order was the nomination of a Senator. The names of S. F. Wilson and Wm. Garretson were presented to the Convention as candidates, and voted or *viva voce*, each delegate naming the candidate of his choice. The first ballot resulted as ollows :

S. F. Wilson, 42. | Wm. Garretson, 24.

Whereupon the President declared Mr. Wilson duly nominated for the office of Senator, subject to the decision of the Senatorial Conference.

Whereupon the President declared Mr. Wilson duly nominated for the office of Senator, subject to the decision of the Senatorial Conference.

L. P. Williston, Joel Parkhurst, and A. Humphrey* were presented as candidates for Representative. Mr. Williston received the nomination on the first ballot as follows:

L. P. WILLISTON, 44.
A. HUMPHREY, 17.
J. PARKHURST 5.

The President then declared Mr. Williston duly nominated for the office of Representative, subject to the decision of the Representative Conference.

On motion of A. J. Sofield Esq, a committee of five was appointed by the Chair to report resolutions expressive of the sentiments of the Convention. I. M. Bodine, Mart. King, J. L. Miller, H. S. Hastings and John Dickinson were appointed as that committee.

On motion the Convention adjourned to allow the committee time to draft the resolutions. After the expiration of the time allowed to the committee the Convention was called to order, and the President announced that the next business in order would be the nomination of a candidate for the office of Treasurer. The names of Jas. S. Watrous of Gaines, Benj. Vandusen of Chatham, V. Case of Knoxville, and H. B. Card of Sullivan were then submitted as candidates. After the first ballot, Benj. VanDusen's name was withdrawn. The balloting was as follows:

Ballots,	1.	2.	3.	4.	5.	6.	7.	8.	9.
JAS. S. WATROUS,	23	19	20	20	22	23	22	27	33
V. CASE		16	19	19	20	18	18	16	12	5
H. B. CARD,		24	27	26	26	25	25	25	25	27
BENJ. VANDUSEN 3										

Mr. Jas. S. Watrous was then declared nominated by *one* majority.

Sofield Poem
January 9, 2014

One day while I was talking to Scott Gitchell at the Historical Society I was looking through his pamphlets, et cetera, and I came across this interesting poem that a contemporary gentleman wrote about the townspeople at that time.

When reading the poem, you can get a feeling of the cohesiveness that the folks of that day had for one other. Don't think that I am walking around with a pink cloud over my head because I know that there had to be some bad apples back then just like there are now—maybe just not as many.

Rather, from this poem, I get the feeling that they all knew each other and there was a semblance of respect going on here. I hate to be redundant, but so far, the way I perceive it, that poem could have been written today, about today's Wellsboro contemporaries with the same respect.

Many people will feel that I am romanticizing this place a little too much, but I seem not to be the only person that has drawn this conclusion. When I talk to people about my ravings about this place they seem to very much agree with me, with a little trepidation. They have lived here most of their lives, some of them, all their lives, so they have seen the gossipers and maybe a little crime, but to an outsider like me who has not only seen, but been the victim of the dishonesty in others it's a pleasure to surround myself with trustworthy humans.

I've lived in four states, California, Utah, Hawaii and now Wellsboro (to me that's a state) Pennsylvania. So you can take it from there and enjoy this one woman's observations on the townspeople.

Here's a little tidbit for Wellsboro lovers (meaning people who love Wellsboro, not lovers in Wellsboro—I just wanted to clarify that) about these trees, one on The Green and on in front of the old jailhouse which is now the Chamber of Commerce.

The Bicentennial of the County Seat
Wellsboro 1806-2006

"On May 27, 2006 the celebration for the Bicentennial of the creation of Wellsboro as the county seat of justice took place.". It was held on the Green in Wellsboro with a large crowd present.

R. Lowell Coolidge, Esq. a trustee of the Tioga County Historical Society acted as Master of Ceremonies. The three commissioners of Tioga County, Erick Coolidge, M. Sue Vogler and Mark Hamilton, John Dugan, President of the Wellsboro Borough Council and James Daugherty Mayor of Wellsboro also participated in the ceremonies.

Allen L Walker, of Mansfield, Pa., a direct descendant of Benjamin and Mary Wells Morris gave a history of the Morris family and their connection to Wellsboro.

State Representative Matthew Baker presented the governor of the Commonwealth of Pennsylvania Hon. Ed Rendell who congratulated Wellsboro on its historic milestone.

The artist who designed the commemorative glass paperweight of the statue Wynken, Blynken and Nod was present and spoke. There was also the burial of a time capsule with various items from local organizations and schools. Timothy McConnell made the container, and the Tussey-Mosher Funeral Home donated the vault in which it was placed. A plaque was placed on the site of the burial and it is hoped that it will be opened in 3006.

A disease resistant American elm hybrid tree was planted on the Green. It was announced that the huge American elm behind the former Corning Glass Plant (now Osram-Sylvania) is the second largest in the Commonwealth of Pennsylvania. The "Jailhouse elm" is now the fourth largest American elm in Pennsylvania. Although both elms are now within the borough at the time Wellsboro was laid out in 1806, only the "Jailhouse elm" was within its bounds. Both trees are living witnesses to the entire recorded history of Wellsboro. —S.P.G.

Wellsboro Flash Poetry by Asa Churchill

Asa Gildersleeve Churchill takes us on another poetic tour of life in Tioga County in the 1850s. The last issue of the Tioga County Historical Review (Volume 5) carried an article on the eccentric poet who, in his sixties, takes a trip to Niagara Falls and never returns. The family assumed him dead, although in reality he had merely started life anew in Canada eventually marrying twice more even though his "widow" in Tioga County was very much alive. Before leaving Tioga County he had published a series of "Flash Poetry" in which he gives a recitation on many towns and boroughs in the county.

This issue deals with Churchill's writings about Wellsboro, and provides a bit of an insight on the characters that inhabited the borough in his day. Some of them such as Henry W. Williams, Lorenzo Parsons Williston, and Stephen Fowler Wilson, were destined to hold high positions on various state supreme courts. A few persons mentioned would die young or tragically, such as Edward Maynard, James Bryden and Alfred I. Sofield. The latter was among the first Tiogans killed at Gettysburg. Many mentioned lived quiet, simple lives as respected tradesmen and merchants.

This poem was almost certainly written in 1854, since Mark H. Cobb did not become publisher of the Wellsboro AGITA-TOR until July and Edward Maynard, Esq. died on October 30 of that year. 1854 is certainly the date the poem was composed but not the date of its publication. The title page is missing from the original, so no date appears on the publication. The date of 1855 or 1856 seems likely.

Asa Churchill was a shoemaker by trade and often traveled to various parts of Tioga County. He was apparently a friendly and amusing character who enjoyed making up poems about the people and places he visited. The great value of his work lies not in any poetic merit but in the historical insight it gives of both people and places he was describing. The following transcript includes his punctuation, capitals, spellings and misspellings of words and names. Every fifth line is numbered to make notes easier to follow. Page numbers in brackets refer to the page in the original publication, a copy of which is in the collection of the Knoxville Library.

            —S.P.G.

Gibbs, Rutland, Chubbock, all polite,
Pratt, Kelly and Depew.

John D. Sofield and Bodine. ALFReD's BRo.
Were clerking in the merchant line,
To live bright young men of manners fine,
In honor to the land,   460
Taught in our select schools.
Learned in all the modern rules,
Pens and pencils are their tools,
They write the fancy hand.

An ample store of books in style.   465
On the shelves are racked in file,
Foley and Richards with a smile,
Will sell you books to read;
Read them and to fame arise,
Read them and their precepts prize,   470
[Page 30]
Read these volumes and be wise.
Librarians indeed.

Sherwood's grocery in grade,
Cider and good lemonade,
Besides his ample stock for trade.   475
Nuts, Candies, Cakes and toys,
E. R. Black at lower shop,
Where the barber's sign does lop:
He will lather chin and chop,
And shave the bearded boys.   480
The names of carpenters we speak,
Two Cleveland's, Bacon, Dimick, Peak.
Landis Forsythe, every week,
And Bellfare, builders all.
Alexander's harness straps,   485
Will draw the buggies and the chaps,
And lots of ladies too, perhaps,
In Independence Ball.

C. H. Koon's and Butler print,
Root and Sturrick in the mint,
Their little devil not of flint,
And yet some precious stone.
Sears and Riley each a shop,
Boots with red morocco top,
For service, fancy and the fop,
Nine Jones are on the throne.   490

                                                       500

Johnson and Vanantwess hire,
Three Searses, George a young admire,
Mister Mosier's always squire,
Tennerry cordwains all,
[Page 31]
Spirit rappings very droll,
Sears and Riley does control,
Eight that rap on heel and sole,
And also on the ball.   505

Where six merry blacksmiths sing,   510
Where six station'd anvils ring.
All mechanics call them king,
Make tools for every name.
Brown, Gray and Kimble all agree,
Hitchcock and Fiele stand in glee,   515
Muck cries in court, hear ye, hear ye,
Is standing high in fame.

Three living men are in their graves,
Harrison the booker shaves,
Christnot will detect the knaves,   520
Is police of the town,
Lemuel Cleveland stands at par,
McNeal is tending Kimble's bar,
Conway, like a useful star,
And English in renown,   525
Sulky, buggy, wagon, cart,
Miles Crowel and Petrie in the art,
And one about as swift as dart,

John R. Bowin's all the go,
Borst and Bailey Smith ditto,
Bean & Ensworth, Jones & Roe,
And Osgood's in that line.
Robert Roy is druggist store,
Has a thousand things or more,
His window front and glowing door,
Transparent walls do shine.

Mr. Gray in his hardware,
Of patronage has quite his share,
Will wait upon you all with care.
To order and co band.
Another store we do rehearse,
Owner social to converse,
Clothing dry-goods and commerce,
He trusties in the land.

William Bache does lands survey,
A well-known agent of the day,
[Page 28]
Will tell where the warrants lay,
On any plot or plan.
Mr. Morris Joseph P.,
A man of birth and high degree,

In conversation social free,
A harmless pleasant man.

Kimble acts the landlord's part,
Cleaver, Robinson and Hart,
Restricted in the license court,
Strong drinks they dare not sell.
Yet their tables well abound,
With lamb and ham and dainties round,

And all dimentions that are found.
Where landlords ring the bell.

They have the ardent with the drugs,   425
And doom the gin and brandy mugs.
Together with the whisky kegs.
To old Vandeimans land.
For gin is streng and man is frail,
They send the pitcher or the pail   430
To bring the best of Adam's ale,
And keep it pure on hand.

Fellows makes his best effort
For fresh supplies at every court.
And he bears a good report,   435
And well established fame.
Weed & Chubbec we are told.
In the foundry melt and mould,
Turn pot-metal into gold,
As traders do the same.   440

[Page 29]

Wilcox keeps the livery stock,   *Dies wl Sofield*   —
In the harness will not balk;
Either run or trot or walk;
Or drive them as you will.
The fields will plaster of your hall;   445
Two win gates open through the wall,
The root is bottom of it all,
Like mason men of skill.
Bache and Ross have quit their store.
To count their gold and silver o'er,   450
The clerks in town are half a score.
Their names we bring to view;
Alansen Donaldson is right,
Chandler, Gibbins, Green a bright,

Property Sell-Off
January 9, 2014

The following pages show some property that my great-grandmother had to sell off to pay debts. This was three months after A.J. was killed. It is so sad that when a spouse dies, or for that matter, anyone with important duties in a family, not only leave you missing that person's love, devotion and companionship, but you leave them with having to make their own decisions on important things that it takes to raise children, pay the bills, et cetera.

The following document shows what she had to go through to get some of those bills paid off, including, I am sure, paying the property taxes. She had to get rid of property and start her own business. My heart breaks when I think of what she had to go through.

	Term 1864 Matter of the Petition of	)	
No. 11			

Helen M. Sofield, Admx   ）   June 11 1864
Upon filing the petition of
of A. J. Sofield dec'd for the   ）   Helen M. Sofield,
Administratrix of the Es-
sale of real estate   ）   tate of A. J. Sofield
late of **Tioga County**, [PA]

deceased. Setting
forth that said intestate
died seized in his demesne as of, per of and in the following described lands, to
wit, the equal **undivided one fourth** part of 400 acres of unseated land in
Charleston Township on Warrant No. 1580, Hewes & Fisher, Warranties, which
he held as tenant in common with ___. A. Guernsey, owner of the remaining three
fourths thereof, that the personal estate is insufficient to pay the debts of decedent,
and that it is expedient to sell a portion of the real estate for the payment thereof.

That she has annexed to said petition a schedule of the debts of said decedent,
a statement showing the amount of the personal estate and a schedule showing the
real estate held by said deceased at the time of his decease, and praying the
Court to make an order authorizing her to sell the above described real estate
at administrators sale.   Terms cash on the confirmation of the sale.

Whereupon June 11, 1864, Court decrees a sale and directs that bond be given by the
Administratrix in the sum of six hundred dollars, conditioned for the execu-
tion of the trust according to law. Terms cash on confirmation of sale. By the Court
June 11, 1864   Bond signed by Helen M. Sofield and Henry W.
Williams and
approved by the Court, filed
June 18, 1864   Order of sale issued

September 5, 1864   Order of sale returned executed and the Administratrix
reports,
That in pursuance of the annexed order she did after giving due and legal notice of the
time and place of sale on Friday the 2nd day of September, A.D. 1864, expose the
premises
in the annexed order mentioned to sale at public vendue or outcry at the Courthouse in the Boro of Wellsboro and then and there sold the same to H. W. Williams
for the price or sum of ten dollars, he being the highest and best bidder and that being
the
highest and best price bidden for the same, which sale so made as aforesaid, she
prays may be confirmed to the said purchaser.

December 5, 1864   Report of Sale confirmed *nisi* By the Court

And now, to wit, February 8, 1864, the within report of sale is confirmed and it is
ordered and decreed that the land and premises so reported sold be and remain
to the said vendee **Henry W. Williams**, his heirs and assigns, firm, stable, forever.

By the Court

One of the parcels that she had to sell to pay debts. SE corner of Central and Walnut.

Wellsboro From Way Back When
January 11, 2014

Main Street, Wellsboro, Pa. – East Side.

The picture on the previous page shows Wellsboro as I imagine that it looked when my family was walking around town. A.J. going to the courthouse, hobnobbing with his political friends along with the real estate buying and selling amongst them all. This part is sad, but I picture Helen at home, wishing that he were present by the home fires more: less business, more family.

She had three little boys to care for and he even refers to himself as a poor husband in a quote from him that I found in a book titled "Courage Under Fire" by Wiley Sword. (This book and passage appears in the second January 16th entry.) He, in the throes of "the blues" as he put it, admitted to not being the ideal husband. What a pity that he wasn't allowed to go back and mend his ways.

Also in this picture I imagine seeing her walking around town with three little boys in tow, shopping for them, probably in some of the same buildings that I shop in now. Then after his demise, I picture more of a sadness…a woman amongst other women that were also widows of that terrible war, trying to find their way in life. I imagine them all trying to find a shoulder to cry on, but finding it hard because they were all looking for the same thing.

When I walk to town, I really do try to imagine these things. I'm steeped in sadness on one hand and thrilled with having to be in the same place as they were. Bittersweet, indeed.

Visiting the Mansfield
Soldiers Orphans School Site
January 9, 2014

Today I decided that I would go to Mansfield
where my Grampa went to the Mansfield Soldiers
Orphans School. It was very cold out but I had to go and
see what my Grampa, you know, the one with the skinny
legs, big middle and brass spittoon, saw when he was
growing up. I try to picture this. Here is this little boy
whose dad had been gone for almost a year and then he
finds out that he won't be coming home.

There are discrepancies in his age when he was in
the orphanage. One 1870 census has him born in 1852
and the other one has him born in 1855, so without
worrying about that difference, we will suppose that he
was between five and eight when he had to also leave his
mother and go to this strange school with other boys and

girls who probably weren't very happy. They also were considered orphans and now away from their parents, too. I don't visualize a lot of happy and joyous little kids in that home.

I stood on the sidewalk in front of the building that replaced the school—which had burned down several years ago. I imagined that I saw him walking on that same corner where I stood, maybe to the store down the street. I was surprised to find that it is on a corner right in the middle of town.

I then went down the street to visit Joyce Tice, who has a huge web site about the three counties here. She had gone home with a bad cold so I didn't get to see her. That pretty much ended my day. The next day, the 10th, had some disappointments in it so we will leave it at that.

A Bit About Roger and Shane
January 12, 2014

I woke up this morning with the intention of responding to the invitation to the Presbyterian Church Service that I had received via email from Roger Wagner. He is the man that created the Civil War Round Table that I attended last Wednesday evening. He is a very average type man, very pleasant, calm of spirit but wouldn't stand out in a crowd—that is, until he gets a microphone in front of an audience. In his email invitation he added that he was going to have the opportunity of presiding over the services today, as the regular minister is in Thailand on a mission. He also mentioned that he was going to interweave the Civil War in his sermon. That really got me interested and interesting
it was.

Roger Wagner

Have you ever known someone that doesn't necessarily stand out in a crowd but onstage they come alive? That is Roger Wagner. He is a born speaker. He enters levity in it, encourages companionship among the congregation and shows a familiarity with those he knows in the group.

He spoke of a couple of different battles in the war making it obvious that he was very well read in that War. He spoke, also, about how there was brother against brother culminating with two of the soldiers, one dressed in blue and the other one dressed in gray, having a bite to eat together on a rock wall. This seemingly took place right after Grant and Lee had brought an end to the devastation that had gone on for four years. He showed how God wasn't ready to bring peace to the world quite yet and that man has to wait until HE is ready.

Whether one believes this way or not, it gave one food for thought. After the sermon there was to be a gathering in another room that included coffee and goodies but I had already made a luncheon appointment with my computer helper, Shane Cleveland at Harlands Restaurant.

Shane Cleveland and me.

While we were waiting for our food to come I looked across the room and a lady came in by herself and sat at a booth. She was about my age but her hair was beautiful, thick and pure white, or should I say silver. So while Shane was trying to make my iPad behave itself, I took it upon myself to go across the room and tell her how beautiful her hair is.

Of course she demurred and then admitted that she had been and still is, to a lesser degree, a beautician.

Her name is Gerry Bassney and lives about ten or so miles from here in a town named Tioga. She said that she would do my hair if I wanted her to as she has a solon set up in her home for a few of her friends. I am going to make an appointment and go get the perm that will finally do what's left of my hair in. She is a very pretty and pleasant lady like all the people that I have met out here. I want to see if Tioga meets with the charm that Wellsboro has.

Please…other shoe, stay put…don't drop!

Gettysburg Dedication
January 13, 2014

We all have heard about President Lincoln giving the Gettysburg Address, but how much more interesting and informative it is to read it from a contemporary newspaper article giving us details of more of a personal nature. I believe that this came from a newspaper called the "Inquirer," although I am not sure which town or state it came from. In my Google search it appears that it was from a Philadelphia newspaper by that name. This article shows the welcoming of President Lincoln as he got off the train in Gettysburg. It also gives us some insight of his humor when he gave a little impromptu speech.

Mr. Lincoln very much hated impromptu speaking, as he was a perfectionist in what he portrayed to his listeners. I truly believe that you will find this article very interesting as it makes you feel as if you were right there. It's much better to read it from a newspaper of that day than to read a report on it from someone else's observations.

On this day, just four months and eighteen days after my great-grandfather was killed, the President arrives in Gettysburg to assist in dedicating the grounds that is to be where the fallen will rest. There were many that were killed on those three days of battle whose families wanted the bodies shipped home and buried where they could come and pay their respects at will. Those of you that have visited this cemetery have seen that it looked like the majority stayed there, all toll 1875 dead soldiers, including 10 rebels.

I used to wonder if my great-grandmother was there at that dedication, but since that time I read in the book, *Courage Under Fire* by Wiley Sword, that in 1864 Helen made plans to visit Gettysburg to see for herself the site where Alfred fought and also his grave. That shows that she didn't make it to the dedication but I always wonder if she ever made it at all because four months later the local Wellsboro newspaper shows her starting her own business.

"Well, Gr-gramma," I wish I could say to her, "even though it has been 135 years later, your great-granddaughter, great-great-granddaughter and great-great-great-granddaughter made that belated visit in 2008." That is when Leslie, my daughter, Kyra, her granddaughter and I took that trip and honored his memory. It was bittersweet.

The wonderful thing about actually living here in Wellsboro is that it brings alive my imagination…especially living so close to where they lived and worked. I imagined her making an effort to get to Gettysburg but I really don't, at this point, think that she ever made it there. Please, if you will, read this article (beginning on the next page) as it really makes that day come alive.

THE GETTYSBURG CELEBRATION.

Additional Details of the Ceremonies.

ORIGIN AND DESCRIPTION OF THE CEMETERY.

Names of Pennsylvanians Reinterred in the Cemetery.

APPEARANCE OF THE BATTLE-FIELD.

Scenes and Incidents in and Around Gettysburg During the Celebration.

PRESIDENT LINCOLN'S SPEECH BEFORE THE DEDICATION.

Special Correspondence of the Inquirer.

GETTYSBURG, Pa., Nov. 18th, 1863.

The nation is writing its own history. The events transpiring in the land render names hitherto obscure and unknown, forever historic. The localities which have been made the theatre upon which the grand events of the present struggle have been enacted will be perpetuated in song and story while the memory of America lasts, or the records of her fame endure.

The tide of battle, whose crimson wings meandered the plains of other States, left the peaceful fields of the Keystone undisturbed by the destruction and ruin which carried the impress of the power of war to homes that never before had known other sounds than the busy din of industry. The glens of Pennsylvania gave back no answering battle shout. The fertile plains were unsullied by the foeman's tread, and while her sons wrote the story of Pennsylvania's loyalty and patriotism in other States, the children of the grand old Commonwealth never fought for their own liberties around their own hearthstones. When the tide of war, fifteen months ago, rolled its advancing waves to our shores, its receding waters ebbed away too rapidly to leave a trace behind. Antietam's hill looked down on the invading hosts as their broken columns slowly trailed towards the Potomac.

But when the great forward movement of the Rebel leaders was made last summer, a foothold sure and strong was gained upon our soil. The expulsion of an army whose arrogance claimed the occupation of the Commonwealth's Capital, and the possession of her Metropolis, could be accomplished but on her own plains. The armies of the South lay encamped in the streets and on the outskirts of the little obscure town of Gettysburg, about one hundred miles southwest of Philadelphia. A quiet country village, embosomed in a circle of high hills, that broke the force of the northern tempest, and stayed the hot blast of the southern winds, it was noted for its picturesque scenery, the unusual fertility of its farmlands, and the hospitality of its inhabitants. Other reputation than that gained from these sources it had none, but the events of the first three days in last July rendered it memorable and historic forever.

The Perpetuation of the Battle-Field.

The circumstances of the three days' struggle in and around Gettysburg are too well known to need republication. The greatest battle of the war was fought among its hills, and the proudest name the ration wrote upon its banners was the name of the little village in Adams county, in the southern part of Pennsylvania. It was Pennsylvania's battleground, the only portion of her soil upon which her sons and the sons of other portions of the sisterhood of States and the pride of the State were interested to preserve the distinctive features of the battle-ground as perfect as possible. The redoubts and intrenchments erected upon the field were proposed to be continued by facings of stone and by substantial, compact sods of earth.

In addition to this project, it was suggested to dedicate a portion of the ground to the manes of the brave men who fell in the triple days' contests, and to consecrate it to them as a National Cemetery, in which the remains of those who, in life, had enjoyed such intimate communion, could repose together in the locked confines of the grave.

Origin of the National Cemetery.

On the 24th day of July last, Mr. DAVID WILLS, of Gettysburg, conceived the idea of establishing a National Cemetery on the grounds near the cemetory at Gettysburg, which has lately played such a conspicuous part in the great battles of the first, second and third days of July last, for the purpose of interring, in a proper manner, the remains of all the Union soldiers who fell in the conflicts alluded to, and whose remains were roughly buried in the fields and on the hills comprising the battle-field.

Mr. WILLS wrote to Governor CURTIN on the subject, who heartily entered into the proposed plan, and offered to render all the aid in his power towards the accomplishment of said object. A variety of correspondence ensued between the parties on the subject, and it was subsequently determined to address the Governors of the different loyal States, and place the whole affair on a broad national basis.

About this time a proposition was made by other parties in Gettysburg, to have the soldiers who fell in the above battles buried within the grounds proper of the Gettysburg Cemetery. This proposition created for a time some difficulty, as it would materially interfere with the plan proposed by Mr. WILLS to create a National Cemetery.

After the lapse of a short time the other proposition was withdrawn, and the work of creating a National Cemetery steadily progressed.

It was decided, on full consultation with the Governors of the other States, that the amount for the purchase of the ground, transferring the bodies, erecting a monument, and other expenses, should be limited to thirty-five thousand dollars, to be apportioned among the States, according to their representation in Congress.

Description of the Cemetery.

The ground purchased for the Cemetery contains seventeen acres, and lies directly north of the old burial ground. It is a narrow strip of land, forming an obtuse angle, and was occupied during the battle by the Union forces, consisting of the left wing of General MEADE's Army.

Desperate charges were made by the Rebels to obtain possession of this ground, but in each instance they were driven back with fearful loss. The plan of the Cemetery is at once original and striking. The portion devoted to the graves is in the form of a semicircle, and it is divided into compartments for the fallen soldiers of each State, said compartments varying in size according to the number to be buried from the several States. In order to give a familiar illustration of the plan of the Cemetery, we may state it somewhat resembles the plan of a tier of boxes in a theatre, with the exception of the irregularity in size of the compartments.

The number of deceased Union soldiers who will ultimately find a final resting place in the National Cemetery will probably reach three thousand. There have already been reinterred, or will be in a day or two, the following number, with the States to which they belong:—

New York	600	New Hampshire	40
Pennsylvania	415	Connecticut	85
Massachusetts	180	Minnesota	20
Ohio	125	Rhode Island	20
Michigan	100	Maryland	15
Maine	85	Delaware	10
Indiana	70	Virginia	10
Vermont	55		
Wisconsin	50	Total	1875
New Jersey	45		

Names of Pennsylvanians Reinterred.

We append below the names of the Pennsylvania soldiers reinterred up to the present time:—

ROW A.

Robert McGum, Co. F, 53d Regiment.
Sergeant Daniel Harrington, Co. F, 53d Regiment.
C. Herbeter, Co. C, 99th Regiment.
Frank'in Myers, Co. D, 99th Regiment.
Thomas Hain, Co. K, 99th Regiment.
Isaiah Butterworth, Co. E, 114th Regiment.
Thomas Burns, Co. B, Second Penna. Reserves.
Thomas Savage, Co. H, Second Penna. Reserves.
Color-Sergt. John Greenwood, Co. I, 109th Regt.
J. Bainbridge, Co. F, 147th Regiment.
G. Deisroth, Co. F, 147th Regiment.
Captain Abraham Crawley, Co. A, 68th Regiment.
Sergeant John Morgan, Co. G, 99th Regiment.
John McIntyre, Co. G, 69th Regiment.
Robert Lockhart, Co. K, 29th Regiment.
Theodore Saylor, Co. C, 72d Regiment.
Lieut. J. D. Gordon, Co. B, 56th Regiment.
Alex. Creighton, Co. F, 143th Regiment.
Sergeant R. H. Cowpland, 121st Regiment.
J. J. Finnefrock, South Huntington, Westmoreland county, Pa.
Samuel Finnefrock, South Huntington, Westmoreland county, Pa.
[The above are supposed to be brothers from letters and d.ary found on them.]
Corporal C. Walters, Co. C, 112d Regiment.
Corporal Jas. S. Gutihns, Co. D, 150th Regiment.
Nathan H. ——, Co. A, 149th Regiment.
F. E Northrop, Co. F, 150th Regiment.
W. H. Harman, 149th Regiment.
James Clay, Co. G, 69th Regiment.
James Coyle, Co. G, 63th Regiment.
James Rice, Co. G, 69th Regiment.
William Kiker, 72d Regiment.
John Hope, Co. H, 71st Regiment.

ROW B.

Capt. A. J. Sofield, Co. A, 149th Regiment.
George Scip, 143th Regiment.
David C. Kline.
Sergt. Philip Peckens, Co. F, 141st Regiment.
Robert Morrison, Co. A, 69th Regiment.
Corp. Samuel Heyburn. Co. B, 103th Regiment.
Samuel K. Garvin, Co. E, 72d Regiment.
John McHugh, Co. K, 72d Regiment.
Ira Corbin, Co. D, 145th Regiment.
H. S. Thomas, Co. I, 145th Regiment.
J. Taylor, Co. G, 145th Regiment.
S. Shoemaker.

ROW C.

H. M. Kensil, Co. H, 110th Regiment.
Chas. T. Gardner, Co. H, 110th Regiment.
Hiram Woodruff, Co. G, 1st Bucktails.
P. O'Brien, Co. A, 69th Regiment.
John Har'ey, Co. H, 69th Regiment.
Geo. Dunkenfield, Co. H, 69th Regiment.
Wm. Evans, Co. I, 71st Regiment.
David Stainbrook, Co. E, 72d Regiment.
Wm. W. Clark, Co. A, 72d Regiment.
Wm. Brown, Co. B, 71st Regiment.

ROW D.

Calvin Porter, Co. H, 149th Regiment.
Corp. Sam. M. Caldwell, Co. D, 118th Regiment.
Frederick Shoner, Co. E, 72d Regiment.
Sergeant Jer. Boyle, Co. H, 69th Regiment.
Geo. Herpich, Co. H, 71st Regiment.
Corp. James McManus, Co. D, 69th Regiment.
Jas. Gallagher, Co. H, 71st Regiment.
Sergeant J. Gallagher, Co. D, 69th Regiment.
S. S. Odare, Co. F, 71st Regiment.

The Period of The Dedication.

The date fixed for the dedication of the Cemetery, was the 19th of November, and the preparations made for the proper celebration of the ceremonies were extensive and universal. The Governors of the different States were invited to participate, and invitations were extended to various delegations and associate bodies throughout the Union. To all these, cordial and willing responses were received. The approach of the day brought visitors from every part of the country. The trains on the different railroads leading to the town were laden with passengers, and standing room could not be obtained in any of the cars. The railroad arrangements were of the most imperfect character. Detention met the passenger at every station, and the correspondents of THE INQUIRER who left the city at eight o'clock on Tuesday morning, reached Gettysburg at ten in the even'ng.

The town was rapidly filling with people. From every direction interminable trains of every variety of vehicles, were found tending towards the town. Every bed in the hotels was occupied. The Seminary and College were converted into temporary sleeping barracks. The churches had the pews transferred into berths and every private house was crowded with lodgers. They were accompanied variously. The ladies of course monopolized the beds and the gentlemen deemed themselves fortunate in securing a mattress and a blanket on the floor of a little chamber occupied by about twenty boarders.

A Crowded Village.

With every train the arrivals increased. The States sent large delegations, and the hotels bore placards, containing the inscriptions:—Head-quarters of Ohio; head-quarters of New Jersey, &c. New York, Massachusetts and other States were represented by large delegations, and corporate bodies sent committees to the dedication. The City Councils of Boston had a large committee on the ground, which reached Gettysburg on Tuesday evening. Wednesday dawned clear, bright and beautiful. The clouds hung lowering over the sunset sky the previous evening, and the rain drops patted merrily down during the early morning watches, but when the grey dawning broke the clouds rolled away and the sunbeams, pleasant and bright, lay along the macadamized street, and glinted adown the curious dwellings of the village. When breakfast was over, thousands turned out from their houses to inspect the battle-grounds and the cemetery. Every horse and carriage in the place was hired at exorbitant rates, and all day long the crowds passed to and fro in ceaseless promenades.

The position occupied by the Confederates during the first day's action was to the west of Gettysburg, and when the Union armies retreated they passed through and around the village to the south, where the succeeding contests were fought. These fields presented the most attractions to the visitors, and were thronged from morn till evening.

Appearance of the Battle-ground.

The appearance of the hills to the south of the town indicate the fearfulness and the tenacity of the struggles which waged around them. Torn knapsacks, cartridge boxes, fragments of clothing, discarded shoes and rejected equipments were scattered over the whole ground. The remains of the horses which had fallen were seen in heaps of charred and mouldering bones, where the fires that consumed them had been kindled. Scabbards and sheaths lay all along the route of the battle, and under the faded, withered autumn leaves the bleached remnants of a thousand letters, the contents of fallen soldiers' knapsacks, were peeping.

The fences in the vicinity had been constructed of stones, and the granite blocks had been carried by our armies and piled in a long range along the apple orchard, through which PICKETT's division of Rebels charged, to waste away before the withering fire of the Union infantry. The rifle-pits on the upper side of the pike were also visited. They were simply mounds of earth, about four feet high, and the same in thickness, reaching from twenty to thirty feet in length. They bore evidences of the deadly fire of artillery that was poured upon them, for their faces were torn and ploughed, and an old, dilapidated tenantless frame building, standing to the southeast of the rifle-pits, was riddled with balls, nearly every window frame being shattered with bullets.

The houses in the town are all more or less marked by balls. Conversing with a gentleman who witnessed the first day's engagement from his housetop, he stated that while there his chimney was perforated by a round shot, and a couple of shells crossed his garret. The residences are scarred and battered, and in one instance a shell, which bored a large hole in the side of a house, had been replaced in the aperture and the bricks built up around it. At the southern end of the town, on the main street, a house stands which is full of bullet holes, and limbs of trees are torn and rent by flying missiles.

The Scene from Cemetery Ridge.

From the cemetery ground the scenery presented is exceedingly interesting, and the view ranges unbroken for miles around the horizon. On all sides lofty hills in clear outlines are defined against the blue sky; then woody crests, standing out in bold relief against the intermediate scenery. The progress of the latter can be traced with perfect readiness from the marbled walls of the college buildings and the seminary, on the northwest, to the high ridges of Culp's Hill, on the east. Three miles away to the south, Round Top towers, and waving tree in

Continued on the Second Page.

The Cemetery and a Confederate Flag
January 15, 2014

I woke up this morning to a light snow falling and it was beautiful. I had a lot of things to accomplish today so I had to create a To Do List.

One of the items on the list was to go to the cemetery and take pictures of my great-great-grandparents tombstone. That cemetery is really beautiful. It is on rolling hills. Most cemeteries are on level ground, but I prefer the hilly look of this one. It even has a log cabin on it. I had called ahead to the keeper of the cemetery to ask where I could find my great-great-grandparents' tombstones and, because he explained it to me very plainly, I found it after a short while.

John Sofield died in December 4, 1860. What ran through my mind was that it was a good thing that he died before his son Alfred was killed at Gettysburg only three years later. John was only fifty-eight when he died. The name next to his was his wife and my great-great-grandmother Julia Weeks Sofield. She died on June 6, 1867, four years after her son was killed. She was only sixty years old when she died.

The entrance to the cemetery

I am glad to see that Julia lived to help my great-grandmother when her husband was killed. I am assuming that she helped, even though they were both certainly in mourning. When you get so deeply involved, as I have, with doing your genealogy, and especially when you are living where they lived, it sometimes get frustrating and even a little sad that a lot of what you reduce to paper is your imagination filling in the blanks. I imagine them crying together. I imagine then trying to explain it to the three little boys who would never see their

father again. I imagine my great-grandmother taking care
of the one son that was still living at home as the other
two boys went to the Veterans Orphans Home in
Mansfield.

My great-great-grandparent's grave site

There was a flag on the tombstone that was put in
a flag holder. On the flag holder was a metal star, such as a
Sheriff's Badge would look, but it was so rusted over that
I couldn't make out what it said on it. I then drove
around the cemetery and looked for a like star that maybe
had not been there as long and I found one that was a
green color with GAR (Grand Old Republic) on it. Here
is what Wikipedia says about it: "The Grand Army of the
Republic (GAR) was a fraternal organization composed of
veterans of the Union Army, US Navy, Marines and
Revenue Cutter Service who served in the American Civil

War. Founded in 1866 in Decatur, Illinois, it was dissolved in 1956 when its last member died. Linking men through their experience of the war, the GAR became among the first organized advocacy groups in American politics, supporting voting rights for black veterans, lobbying the US Congress to establish veterans' pensions, and supporting Republican political candidates. Its peak membership, at more than 490,000, was in 1890, a high point of Civil War commemorative ceremonies. It was succeeded by the Sons of Union Veterans of the Civil War (SUVCW), composed of male descendants of Union veterans."

I noticed that GAR wasn't established until three years after Gettysburg but it still applied. What I don't understand is why it was on my great-great-grandfather's grave. The only thing that comes to mind is that the Mexican/American War was between 1846 and 1848. That would have made John forty-four when that war happened so I haven't found that out yet.

I called the VFW and they aren't the ones who put these flags on the graves. They told me to call the American Legion but no luck there...yet! I found out where their office is and I'll go searching soon. The VFW told me that the Boy Scouts also do this on Memorial Day. I have stumbled onto another little mystery for me to snoop around and solve.

The next discovery really surprised me. Right next door from the cemetery was a home with a flag waving bravely in the breeze...but I had to take a second look to believe my eyes: it was a Confederate Flag.

The Confederate Flag in a Wellsboro Yard

I thought that was tacky to put right next to a cemetery that was full of graves of Union men that had died in the Civil War.

Personally I am not a lover of war...but that war seemed to me to be the closest war with a necessary outcome: an outcome for thousands of African-Americans who didn't have the freedom that we attribute to all our wars. I know that Lincoln's main issue was keeping the states united but he hated the idea of slavery also and worked it right into that theme.

I look around at today's racial issues and try to compare them with the issues of the 1800s and I do believe that the laws have come a long way, but in the hearts of many people, sadly, it hasn't. I just couldn't believe that right here in this adorable little town there waves a flag of hate. If there are others in this town that feel empathy with this outlook or philosophy, I hope that I don't meet them. Whether you love or hate President Obama, the fact that we have a president that is half black tells me that we have come a long way.

A Society, a Game and Some Donuts
January 16, 2014

This morning I wasn't feeling very well. It seems that I had too many cobwebs in the brain. By the time the day was over, I felt much better—you will see why when you read this.

Most of my new knowledge from today came via telephone calls. The lady who did my hair the other day, Gerry Bassney from Tioga, heard my story and called me yesterday telling me that she had given my phone number to a lady named Mary Wise Janeski. Mary liked my story and called me and told me that there is a senior center here and that I should go over there. (I went there and it was closed today.) She said that there are a lot of people whose families have been here for years and that they will surely know something. What people don't realize is that we are talking about the 1800s and I really don't think that there is anyone here that knows anyone from that era.

The only time you find that happening is if there is a Civil War link: a relative's ancestor went into the army at the same time and was also from Wellsboro, et cetera.

Mary then invited me to go to a little get together that she and some other friends have every Thursday night at Dunkin' Donuts, and at 10PM! I thought that was funny, both the time <u>and</u> the place. If I am awake at that time I just may go....right after I go to Trivia Night from 7-9PM. She also gave me the names of others that I could call for information.

The current, abandoned railroad station

I rode around a little before visiting the Historical Society and ran into the railroad station that I had been wondering about. It is on Cane Street. The picture above is the one that is there now. When I later asked Scott at the Historical Society about it he said that the one there now has since been abandoned—even though there is a freight train that passes through now and then.

I peeked in the windows and I could tell that it hasn't been used in a long time. Scott said that the location of this newer building is approximately where the one from the 1800s stood. It is also where my great-grandmother most likely went to New York for her millinery business.

When I was with Scott Gitchell at the Historical Society, I must have asked him a dozen questions. I asked him if some of the stores that are now in town were there back then and he showed me a picture of it back then and pointed to the Penn Hotel which is here now. Then he showed me two homes right by it in the commercial district and told me who lived in them back then. He is a wealth of knowledge. He did say, though, that there might be about two commercial buildings that are still standing besides the Penn Hotel. I was a little disappointed: I was hoping that the whole little town was as they saw it....but....it's not to be. While there, I purchased a booklet that tells all about the establishment of Wellsboro back in the late 1700s. It tells of the settlers, et cetera. I hope to find some good information in there.

I came home and fixed something to eat and thought that I would sit down and start reading this booklet. It is called *A Compendium of Events and History of Tioga County*. It was written by The Honorable Judge Charles G. Webb who was the Judge of Tioga County from 1951-1972. The booklet has 67 pages and is on 8 ½ X 11 paper with a soft cover. Besides the history of Wellsboro on the first thirty-seven pages, many old and new pictures follow. This booklet was first printed in 1965 and updated in 1973.

I sat down at 5:30 PM and thought that I would read until 6:45 PM and then go to my Thursday Trivia Night that is held at the Timeless Restaurant and Bar from 7PM – 9PM, but here's what *actually* happened: I kept trying to put the booklet down but when I looked at the clock it was 7:45 PM!

Anyone that is interested in the Wellsboro beginnings and the evolution of the concept of it, the geographical plan of it (it was patterned after Philadelphia) and anyone from different areas that made the trip here to actualize it has to read this booklet. The details in this booklet are amazing. The author shows the names of the people that first built log cabins here in 1800 and what was standing in those parcels back in 1972. I was really amazed that once Wellsboro started having folks moving here, that the first area of population was between Central Avenue, then known as The Avenue, over to King Street and in the other direction from Water Street back to Walnut Street. I live on Main Street and that is right in the middle. **I was happy to realize that is exactly where I live:** on Main Street, right in the middle

I strongly suggest that anyone interested in the history of Wellsboro go to the Historical Society and buy this booklet. It's worth the $9.95 that it costs.

When I came to my senses and looked at the clock I knew that I was already late for my Trivia game. I rushed around and got there late and they were still playing. I found a table that had an empty spot and asked if I could join them and they said that, of course, I could. There was one young woman named Heather and her husband

Tom Lungren and another young man named Bryn Dunham and next to me was Adam Heitzenadter.

Adam was really funny. I told them that they were going to get the benefit of age (me) at their table. The very first question was, "What is the Remington2?" They started murmuring aloud about a gun and then a razor. I spoke up and said, "You don't really think that they are going to be that obvious do you?" So they asked me what I thought that it was so I told them that when I was a teen-ager I had a Remington Typewriter....so they went with that. After everyone in the place sent in their answers, we were the only ones who got it right. You should have heard the yells from our table and then came the high fives. It was so fun. There was one that I got wrong that made me mad at myself and that was, "What city does the Nobel Prize come from for art?" I thought it was Oslo and it turned out to be Stockholm. I hung my head in shame. What a fun night!

Our table won $35 and we decided to put it towards a meal next Thursday when we meet again.

By now it was 9PM and I headed for my next "appointment" which was to be held at Dunkin' Donuts at 10PM. Yes, I went.

I waited for them to come while I read the paper and at about 10PM, they arrived. The lady who invited me, Mary, is an artist and what she does is paint beautiful birds onto Christmas Tree ornament bulbs. They're really pretty. Then another man, Bud Boyce came along and we talked for a while and then two ladies who were sisters came in and one of them got out her paints and started practicing. It turned out that she takes lessons from Mary right there in Dunkin' Donuts at 10:30 PM. Then another two men came in and talked for a while.

I got tired and even though I was having a nice time I thought that it was time that my old self went home and went to bed. That entire evening, plus a few soothing words from my editor via email, greatly improved my already good mood. After reviewing my emails, I watched the taped *American Idol* show until midnight and then slept, slept, slept with a smile.

A.J. Sofield's Letters

January 16, 2014

The following is a *"Courage Under Fire"* by Wiley Sword excerpt from the last letter that AJS wrote to his wife, Helen, before he was killed two weeks later.

"Captain Alfred J. Sofield of the 149th Pennsylvania Infantry, one of the famous Bucktails units, had left his wife, Helen, and three young children behind in Tioga County, Pennsylvania in 1861 (sic) *(it was 1862)*. A former justice and county official at Wellsboro, Pennsylvania, Sofield was a highly regarded and effective administrator and was known for his levelheaded competence. It seemed highly unusual for Sofield to emotionalize in a letter to his wife, as he did on June 3rd, 1863, when he admitted: *I have the blues worse than ever. To be reminded (by a letter from home) that I was so necessary to your happiness, and feeling far short of my duty as a husband as I have been for the past 12 years, and how indulgent and forgiving you have been, causes me to feel sad, indeed....If I am permitted to join you again after getting out of this war, I will try to atone for past errors.*

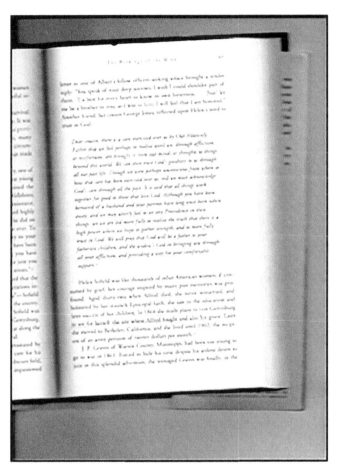

A page from Courage Under Fire

Aware that important events were pending, he wrote: *It is supposed that the Rebels contemplate assuming the offensive and their later operations indicate a movement by them into Maryland and Pennsylvania.* Sofield told Helen that they soon would likely have a big fight with the enemy. Indeed twenty-eight days after writing this letter, Captain Sofield was amidst of horrific combat along Seminary Ridge at Gettysburg. While leading his Bucktails in a charge against the RR cut along the Chambersburg Pike, Sofield went down with a mortal wound.

His wife, Helen, soon learned of his fate and was devastated by grief. Instead of coming home to rekindle their love and care for his family, her husband was consigned to a shallow grave, in an obscure field nevermore to caress his wife or play with his children."

The book goes on to explain another letter that he had written to a bereaving fellow officer, seeking solace, who had just lost a comrade, I assume, in combat,

This is the impassioned letter that he replied: *You speak of your deep sorrows. I wish I could shoulder part of them. Is best for every heart to know its own bitterness…(but) let me be a brother to you, as I was to him; I will feel that I am honored.*

Another friend, "Helen's cousin, George Jones, reflected upon Helen's need to trust in God. He wrote: *Dear Cousin, there is a care exercised over us by Our Heavenly Father that we fail perhaps to realize until we, through affliction, or misfortune, are brought to turn our minds or thoughts to things beyond this world. We can then*

*trace God's goodness to us through all our past life. Though
we were perhaps unconscious from where or how that care
has been exercised over us, still we must acknowledge God's
care through all the past. It is said that all things work
together for good to those that love God. Although you have
been bereaved of a husband and your parents have long since
been taken away and we may utterly fail to see any
Providence in these things, yet we are led more fully to
realize the truth that there is a high power where we hope to
gather strength, and to more fully trust in God. We will
pray that God will be a father to your fatherless children
and the widow's God in bringing you through all your
afflictions, and providing a way for your comfortable
support."*

The book continues: "In 1864 she made plans to
visit Gettysburg to see for herself the site where Alfred
fought and also his grave." I don't believe that she ever
made it there. The book brings out that at age thirty-two,
she never remarried and that she was bolstered by her
Episcopal Faith and that she went on to see the later
successes of her children.   Sad to say, though, the book
doesn't mention the passing of her mother-in-law four
years later, and her twenty-seven-year-old son who had
been a local fireman and was killed in a train wreck. She
had the funeral at her home here on Main Street.

She later managed to move to Illinois to be with
relatives and then on to Berkeley, California, to live out
the rest of her life with her son, William, where she died at
the age of seventy-two.

I feel that I have pretty much figured out A.J.'s and
Helen's personalities. It seems to me that he, like I have

said before, was rather aloof and all business, even rather cool with his children, whereas with her, I believe that she was a non-complaining, suffer-in-silence type of wife. Also looking back at his son, Benjamin, my grandfather, I remember him being much the same type of cool temperament, but without the business sense of his dad. I never saw much of an exchange between him and my gramma, Lillie Belle. I guess we are all pretty complex humans, aren't we?

A Wellsboro Weekend With Brian
Friday, January 17, 2014

Brian arrived here in Wellsboro in the afternoon and he didn't appreciate the snow on the ground. Remember, he likes sand on the ground. He's a beach lover and I'm a snow lover. Since he had just arrived at around 5PM, we decided to go to The Steak House, our favorite place to eat. That restaurant is so popular and cozy.

I got the usual Lamb Steak with mint sauce and he got fish this time. Then, of course, I had to have two of their delicious Margaritas. I do wish, though, that it had been a tad warmer so that we could have done some walking. This is definitely a town where it would be my kind of walking because everything is so close and cozy. Alas, instead of a walk we just came home and talked. He hates TV but we did see the only programs, almost, that he will watch they are Jon Stewart and Stephen Colbert. I guess that may answer any question as to his leanings. If it's not Nova or National Geographic or Bill Maher, forget it. Shortly thereafter, we went to sleep.

Saturday, January 18, 2014

Today Brian and I did some computer work and then took a ride to the cemetery so he could take my picture next to my great-great-grandparent's tombstone. I am wondering if I should use a better word than tombstone. That sounds so Stephen King-ish. How about gravestone or headstone? Yes, I think I shall start saying headstone; that's much better.   I then showed him the Confederate Flag waving as if to say, "I still don't believe that we lost!" That's all I have to say on that subject.

After that we had contemplated going to the show but there wasn't anything showing that he liked so we went to an Italian Restaurant and injested some serious calories. One of the things that he brought back to me here was our bathroom scale~~~~ he's cruel that way. So far I have not approached it, in fact when I walk past it, I go way around it. I don't want to tempt it to beckon me over to it. My best guide are the clothes in my closet that are becoming quite lonely, waiting for me to be able to just slip into them instead of pulling and yanking them.

Brian remains his svelte self. Oh well, he's just a seventy-two-year-old kid. Anyway, after stuffing ourselves we just came home and sat by the fireplace and talked.

Sunday, January 19, 2014

When my sweet landlady heard that Brian was coming for a visit, she gave me a complementary gift card for two to her upscale diner that she owns in Mansfield called Lamb's Creek Food & Spirits. It's for today's brunch at 11AM. I am looking forward to that gathering of Weight Watcher's points.

1PM Sunday

Just got back from the beautiful, upscale Lambs Creek Dining Brunch. That restaurant is absolutely exquisite. The woodwork over the main dining area looked like it had been hand carved, the window looking out the front had a little bird house on which the birds were keeping us entertained while we ate. Then there was the food! The variety was vast. My favorite was the eggs benedict. I had never tasted them the way they made them. Then there was the service. The waitresses walked around with a hot coffee urn on a trey always keeping our coffee hot. All and all we loved it. Even after Brian goes back home I may find my way back there in the future and take a friend with me.

6PM Sunday

Tonight Brian and I just relaxed in front of the fireplace. He has to get up real early while it is still dark and drive back to Bethlehem for an 8AM meeting. Because he will leave when it is still dark, of course, I will worry: that's my job.

The Bottom Drops Out ... Again
January 20, 2014

Well, here we go again. I love when Brian comes to see me but then there is the "bottom drops out" feeling when he leaves. He had to get up at 5AM to get there in time. He runs interference between the property owner(s) and the engineers. What is so disheartening is that the engineers are always late and he has to just sit there in the car and wait for them. I even suggested that he get up later and be a little late but I have known Brian since 1982 and I never seen him late to anything.

As I've mentioned before in this book, Brian hates cold. Anything under 75 degrees to him is cold. This morning when he left it was *bone-chilling* cold. I called him at 7:45AM and he had already gotten there and the engineers hadn't shown up yet. Poor guy.

Today I am going to try to get to Mansfield to see Joyce Tice. I will call her first. Everyone here knows who she is but in case you, the reader, don't know her, here is her website: "TriCounties Genealogy and History." The three counties in that site are Tioga, Bradford, Pennsylvania and Chemung, New York. It is the most comprehensive site I have ever seen and she is continuing to add things. As it stands now there are 15,000 pages in it.

9PM

Well here it is 9PM on Monday night and I had decided that it was just too cold out to even try to go to see Joyce. Besides, I have to fight the short-lived depression after Brian leaves. Once I know that he has returned safely, I can relax.

Rejection
January 23, 2014

As you know, I USUALLY look so forward to
Thursday nights because that's Trivia Night at Timeless
Destinations.

Then last week I sat with a group that was a little
older, I am guessing about late twenties. I asked if I could
join them, because people usually come in with a pre-
arranged group but there was an extra space with a chair at
their table.

Look above at the photograph on the next page
and you will see the two tables behind the two in the
middle. Well, they were pushed together and they said that
I could join them. Well, not to brag, but, of course, we
won again. At the moment I can't remember the
questions that I helped with but we all high-fived and won
$35.00.

Timeless Destinations

I was so anxious to meet with them last night that I even put makeup on. I usually hate to bother but I made an effort. I braved the below-zero weather and drove the three blocks to the restaurant and when I went in, there was the same group, only an extra man was there.

I walked up to the table and there was a space at the end of it with no chair and when I went to get a chair and the same girl that was real friendly the previous week said, "I'm sorry, but we are expecting two more people."

I said, "I thought that we were going to use that $35 towards the food that we were going to order," "I'll just give you your $5.00," she responded.

"Never mind," I said.

I was crushed! There was nowhere else to sit except at the bar. If you look again at the picture you will see the bar right behind the tables. I dejectedly slinked over to the bar and when I would look at any of them I got a blank stare back to me. Not a smile, a nod of recognition, nothing!!

I ordered a diet coke at the bar and considered just going home. Then I stupidly started getting tears in my eyes. It reminded me of when I was in high school and a friend would suddenly and thoughtlessly reject me for some stupid reason and sometimes for no reason, just meanness. It was very immature of me but I felt so rejected. It is the first group—even first person—that I have come across in Wellsboro who was not nice.

I didn't know how to take her actions, her words. Was this planned ahead of time before I got there, that in case I came in she would be the one to tell me not to sit down? I had lost my appetite (that is something that I almost never lose, but when I'm very unhappy the food doesn't taste good.)

As I turned to go, the hostess came up to me and asked me if I needed a partner and I said that I did. She said that a lady that always comes here called and said that the rest of her group wasn't going to make it and that she wanted to know if there was anyone else that she could play with.

"Yes, I'd love that," I said.

I then called Brian and started blubbering on the phone and he said that he felt sorry for me and wished that he was there so he could yell at those people. He wanted to stay on the phone while I cried but I had to hang up and dry my tears.

A few minutes later a very nice lady named Ann Strong came in and we played together there at the bar and we both lost, but that's okay: the questions were harder. (Yeah right, that's my excuse.) I then ordered food and ate and felt better. She even invited me to join their group next week and I, of course, accepted.

Wasn't that a sad story? Are any of you crying yet? Silly me! By the way, those two extra people that were supposed to join that group of twenty-somethings never showed up. I think that it was because there weren't two more people who were supposed to show up. Now you readers, dry your tears because the next day was better.

The Von Trapp Family
January 24, 2014

Today I had more to look forward to. I was invited to go to a Friday's Ladies Day meeting. Yes, you guessed it, it is right across the street next to the library. What a wonderful group of cultured, intelligent ladies. The thing that they do at these meetings is that each lady chooses a subject (usually a person) to write about and gets up and reads what they have written, to the group. It lasts about forty-five minutes. Today's meeting was about the Von Trapp family.

It was so interesting. She had pictures of the whole family starting with the Trapp father and his first wife, who he had seven children with. Then she died of Scarlett Fever during WWI. Then she told how Maria came to live with them and became the children's nanny.

Just like in the movie, they sang. They had been singing even before Maria came to live with them. Maria wanted to become a Nun but the convent told her that God wanted her to go and live with the Von Trapps and she dejectedly did.

I know that most of you have seen the movie *The Sound of Music* and also know that some of the Von Trapp children were upset because the script didn't stick to some of the truths. (SHOCKER!) The presenter had an array of pictures from their early years down to the ones who are still alive—mainly Maria's grandchildren and great-grandchildren who are still traveling and singing.

After that was over we went to the Penn Hotel and had lunch. There were nine of us. Two of them had done their genealogy. One of the ladies had her roots here in Wellsboro also and the other one traced her family back to, as she said, "Jesus." She found that she is related to Charlemagne and other historical figures. She said that most of us are related on some form or other, either directly or indirectly to a historical figure. I wish that I had taken my iPad and taken pictures of us all today but I had left in a hurry and couldn't find it. Next meeting I will do it.

While there, I was invited to go to a Scottish Poetry session this coming Sunday, complete with a Scottish meal, bagpipes playing, and people bringing poetry of their choosing. It is a yearly event honoring Robert Burns, the famous Scottish poet. I want to say that this little town—along with Mansfield—has so much culture and entertainment that I am so glad to be able to spend some of my twilight years in this quaint little town of Wellsboro.

My-Great-Grand Uncle Otis
January 23, 2014

When we curious people do our genealogy we pick up bits and pieces of information along the way and we can't help but to start to draw conclusions about our ancestors. Some people find that their history includes bank robbers, horse thieves, et cetera, and I haven't found that to be the case, as yet anyway. But also there are some that are more colorful than their siblings and I am finding Otis Sofield, Alfred's youngest sibling, was an "interesting" person.

The first thing that I found out about him was that he was drafted into the Army just a few months after Alfred was killed and he paid a substitute to go in his stead. I thought that was very smart for him to do. I'm sure that his mom was happy about that. Then I see that he traveled all over. He lived in Omaha, Nebraska, Nashville, Tennessee, Chicago, Illinois, and maybe more.

This article below will shed a little light on some of the
shenanigans that it looks like he was pulling. Maybe some
of his traveling wasn't alone?! It seems that Mrs. Sofield
hadn't given a thought to the fact that her husband had
disappeared at the same time that their female hotel
worker had gone away. It also looked like the worker had
an alias or two. Read ahead and form your own
conclusion. After all, no one wants a completely boring
history and so far Otis is the only one that seems to fill
that bill.

SHE DON'T BELIEVE THEM

Mrs. Sofield, of the Hotel Bartholdi, Stands by Her Husband.

Otis G. Sofield is absent from Chicago, and
since he went away, a week ago last Thursday,
busy tongues in certain quarters have engaged
themselves with stories concerning the cause
of his departure and some incidents connected
with it.

The story was that he had gone away, leaving
for his wife a note to the effect that he had
ceased to love her, and had gone to make a new
home for a woman he did love, and to whom he
had been married for three years. This Mrs.
Sofield denies point blank, and there seems to
be no foundation for it. He left no letter of
that kind behind him, and there is no evidence
that he is a bigamist, the stories all to the con-
trary notwithstanding.

Mr. Sofield has been a commercial
traveler for about four years, prior to that
time having held department positions
at Washington. He represented at different
times Cribben, Sexton & Co., and Perry & Co.,
and while he was on the road Mrs. Sofield con-
ducted a fashionable boarding-house on Michigan avenue.

In February last, about the 4th or 5th, Mr.
Sofield was employed to manage the Hotel
Bartholdi, and a day or two after his duty com-
menced a Mrs. Ackley was employed as house-
keeper.

To a reporter for THE INTER OCEAN, when asked about the matter, Mrs. Sofield said: "Yes, my husband has gone away, and I have heard a good many stories about his having gone away with a woman, but I don't believe what I don't see, and I have never had any reason to doubt my husband, that I know of. We have been married for twenty-five years, and it would take a good deal to make me think he had cast me off at this late day."

"Do you think, as a matter of fact, that he has gone with another woman?"

"Of course I don't know anything about that. I have heard the stories, and am investigating them somewhat. I have traced them as far as Aurora, and it may be that the story is true."

"Do you know the woman?"

"I have seen her."

"What was her name?"

"Well, that's a hard question to answer.[1] She went by the name of Ackley here, but I understand at different times she has borne the names of Gibson and Powers."

"Do you know when she came to Chicago?"

"Yes; she came here from Elburn about Feb. 7, and went right to work in the hotel."

"Was that after your husband took charge of it?"

"Yes, a day or two."

"Did he hire her?"

"I don't know, but I suppose it was his duty to employ the help."

"You say your husband has been gone more than a week, Mrs. Sofield; has he written to you since he went away?"

"No, he hasn't."

"Is he in the habit of writing home when he is out on the road?"

"Well, up to perhaps a year ago he always wrote regularly. Since then he has not. Since then he has often been gone a month and more without writing at all."

"Has this never aroused your suspicion that something might be wrong?"

"Well, perhaps it did at first, but I got used to it, and made no comment on it."

"As a matter of fact, Mrs. Sofield, what do you think of these stories?"

"Well sir, my husband and I have been married over twenty-five years, and I have never known him to do an ungentlemanly thing. He is forty-eight years old now, and the father of five children, and it seems almost impossible to believe that he would go away and leave us penniless and in this condition. But these stories come to me with a presistence that requires them to be investigated, and I shall give them a thorough examination. I will not believe them until they are proved." . . .   . .

Before leaving home Mr. Sofield indulged in a little financial expedition. It was about in this way: A Mr. Swasey gave a bill of sale of the Hotel Bartholdi furniture and fixtures to Mr. Sofield. Sofield went to Mr. Woodhull, a loan agent at Room 31 Major Block, and secured a loan of $1,050. Then destroying the bill of sale, Mr. Swasey took a mortgage for $1,500 and got it on record about ten minutes before Mr. Woodhull got his into Recorder Scribner's care and keeping. When Mr. Woodhull discovered this, had Mr. Swasey been constructed on the plans and specifications of a feline, the fur would have filled the air. Not being accorded that privilege Mr. Woodhull secured the assistance of an attorney and replevied the stock as well as secured the arrest of Mr. Swasey for conspiracy, whereupon the latter gentleman turned over to the former the prior mortgage, and extricated himself from the complications.

My Scottish Adventure
January 26, 2014

Brrr. It's snowing pretty hard right now. Tonight I went to my first Robert Burns celebration at a restaurant called "The Wren's Nest." I had never heard of that celebration but I had heard of Robert Burns, the Scottish Poet. Reading up about him a bit so that I wouldn't be caught being completely uninformed when I got there, I discovered that he was a hellion of his time and died at age thirty-two.

The celebration was of his birthday and was in Mansfield. It was pretty icy on the road so I kept my 4X4s on just in case. You must remember I was born and raised in Riverside, California, where the sun shines most of the time, and then lived in Hawaii where there is too much sun, so this snow stuff is a novelty for me—just not to drive in. But, I digress.

The above photo is what The Wren's Nest looked like last night and the below photo is how it looked in 1855

When I first arrived at the Wren's Nest, they offered everyone a jigger of Scotch~~~free. I took it and mixed it with a Diet Coke, classy lady that I am. I arrived at just the right time but there were already quite a few people there. I wandered around this beautiful place and looked at all the friendly faces and felt very happy.

I am so impressed with the beautiful homes around here that were built back in the 1800s and have been refurbished.

This was the dining room in 1875. It was built in 1835. (Old pictures taken from the Joyce Tice Website. Thank you, Joyce.)

This is the dining room now from a different angle.

This is what I saw when I came in:

Scottish Trio. Very Nice!!

Pat Davis and I at the table WHERE we ate.

Here's WHAT we ate.

This above photo is of a hard-boiled egg with some sort of a breading around it and then deep-fried, with a mustard sauce. Then there were two (one showing) salmon pieces wrapped around something delicious. That was the first thing that they served. Actually it filled up all of us at the table. Then the next thing that came was soup. Ok, I can down the soup. Then the next dish that came was a salad with some dressing in it that had an anchovy taste to it. It was good, but I was sooo full.

Pat, who sat next to me said, "They haven't even served the main course as yet! Oh my gosh!!…and she was right, because then along came the main dish. It was a liverwurst mixture that looked like turkey dressing and it was good….but I was FULL! Along with that were mashed potatoes, mashed turnips and carrots.

I watched and everyone was just kind of picking at his or her food. After we finished along comes the waitress with dessert! Oh HELP! I usually don't eat the dessert but I certainly wouldn't have wanted to hurt the host's feelings now would I? It was a piece of scotch cake topped with raspberries and whipped cream. It was delicious…so they tell me. I had a wonderful time.

Also at my table was a man named Ryan. He was younger than most of the folks there. Then I found out that he is the editor of the local newspaper, the Gazette. He was just the man I wanted to meet. I asked him if they did news releases and he said that the person that I needed to talk to was Natalie and that he would give her my card and have her call me. I will keep you all abreast as to what becomes of that, if anything.

This following morning, Monday the 27th, I received a phone call from Brian. He told me that his wheels were making a loud clunking sound. I hate those loud clunking sounds! He was going to take it in to a mechanic there in Flemington, New Jersey, where he works. We feared the worst. Later he called me and found out that all of his lug nuts in the front right wheel had been like sheered off. He had one left. That could have been tragic. Two hundred and fifty dollars later it was fixed. Lug nuts in New Jersey are quite expensive!

So So So Cold

January 28 and 29, 2014

The past two days have been freezing. I love
winter, but there is so much that I want to be able to do
outside while getting this book written. I walked across the
street to the Court House yesterday to see if I could get a
fix on Jones in the whole Index Book.

Remember my great grandmother was born and
raised here and in that Compendium book, as I have
already relayed to you: it speaks of Ezekiel Jones. I got a
hint as to where he lived from that book but I wanted to
see the document. Well it turned out to be documents!
There were six (6) real estate transactions in all, three (3)
with Joseph Sofield (I have yet to find out who Joseph
Sofield was, but he had many real estate transactions
through the years) and three that Jones purchased from
the County Commissioner.

This information makes me feel like he was a pioneer in Wellsboro. In one place in the Compendium on Page 11 under the heading "V-Wellsboro-1815-1820" it states, "The total population was probably between 35 and 50, among these a shoemaker, a copper, (a copper? Is that slang for policeman?) a blacksmith, a physician and two shopkeepers. Ezekiel L. Jones was the blacksmith The earliest date on his deeds was August 8, 1815, whereby, in one of the deeds it was where he had purchased it from the County Commissioner….to me, indicates that the little community was setting down stakes to create this little paradise and he was involved in that quest.

Now back to the reason that I would like it to get just a tad warmer: it is so that I can walk to the corner and start walking off the property descriptions. I see from his deeds that he bought and sold property on both sides of Main Street. One property backs up to Pearl Street that is one street behind me and Walnut Street that is two blocks behind me and where my landlady Nelle lives. She's on the corner of Walnut and King. I am anxious to see if perhaps he lived on that same corner or at least owned the property at one time. The map on the following page shows where I live (green arrow)…I am in the heart of where the pioneers of this town began. (I also notice that I am close to a hospital…being the age I am, that makes me feel secure—as you will read later in the book.)

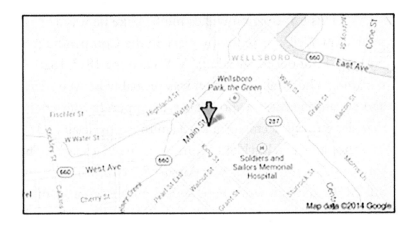

The little shopping portion of the town starts at Central and Main and pretty much stops at East Avenue. No room for a Wal-Mart. We do have a McDonalds, a CVS, Rite Aide, two large grocery stores and a few other local companies. To me, it's perfect just the way it is.

He's Back!

January 30

Well I had a visitor again Thursday evening—and
of all people, my husband. He came here, not to rest, but
to work! His work consists of a lot of telephone and
computer work so that was what was going on most of the
day Thursday. It was still nice to have him here. For some
reason it is cozier when he's here. Of course when you
are alone you get to make decisions that make you
comfortable but when someone else is with you, you have
to make sure that they are also comfortable. Brian and I
are two totally different people. I enjoy the company of
others, although I do like my alone time, too—especially
when I like where I am and I love where I am.

Brian, on the other hand, is very happy to be alone
most of the time. He likes summer, and I like every
season that isn't summer. We both wonder why we are
together and so do a lot of other people, but the surprise

is, is that we have been together for thirty-one-and-one-half years and I am not looking forward to it ending. There've been a lot of obstacles, but also a lot of joy.

Here lies the problem: he will definitely be heading back to eternal summer, complete with cockroaches and centipedes, sand in the bed and never again having to dress up. One doesn't wear make-up; well, one doesn't wear make-up in Hawaii, that is, as it melts off. Back to shorts and flip-flops. I do have a lot of friends there that I played MahJong with about three times per week, and I do miss those people and that game.

When that time comes I have a big decision to make: do I stay in this adorable little town where my ancestors grew up, got married, had businesses and possibly had a part pioneering Wellsboro and the surrounding areas, or do I go to be with my husband whom I love very much? I am trying to take this decision one day at a time, as it's not easy. Brian is also starting a Hawaii business while he is here financing the seed money for it. His business is a local Hawaiian currency that he hopes to get moving when he gets there.

This time, though instead of Maui, he wants us to move to Hilo on the Big Island. He says that it is cooler and he likes it because there are **less** people and traffic and that there will always be food there because there are more wide open spaces and year-round farms for when the bad times hit. I'd like to be two people right now but I really don't think that is going to happen.

January 31, 2014

This morning we got up and put the little fireplace on in the living room and after we warmed up a bit, we decided to go to breakfast. This time we decided to head west instead of east that goes into the little town. We went a whole two blocks, yes, across the street. It's a cute little cozy restaurant named West End Café. The address is 152 Main Street and mine is 133 Main Street. See, I wasn't lying: just across the street only down two blocks. When we first went in we noticed that there were only four tables in there and I believe one outside for summer eating. Everything in there is homemade and healthy, not to mention, delicious.

Governor of Pennsylvania, Edward Rendell, Pam Walker and her brother Allen Walker, Morris - Wells Descendants, at the 200th anniversary of Wellsboro.

Pam, the waitress, waited on us and I, of course, asked her right away if she was from here. Wow, was she EVER!! She is a relative the Wells'. They were the founders of Wellsboro and there is a statue of Mary Wells next to the Courthouse. Wellsboro was named by her dad after Mary, his daughter. Pam is a direct line from them.

Do you remember last week when I talked about the tribute to Robert Burns, the Scotch poet? I have pictures of the restaurant where we had it, before and after pictures? Well Pam was raised in that house. Now *that's* serious ancestry. She knows every inch of this county. I really want to get to know her more and for those of you who aren't from Wellsboro and are vacationing here, be sure to stop there and have a healthy delicious breakfast or lunch.

This is Pam Walker Shipe in the cute little restaurant where she works.

This is a descendent of Pam Walker Shipe,
Mary Wells

Last Wednesday when I got my subscription of the
Gazette in the mail, I started reading it and for some
reason I always read the obituaries. I have done that since
I was a teenager. There, in the obituaries was a picture of
a beautiful cat with two columns telling of his death.
When I started reading it I discovered that he was the
"From My Shelf" bookstore cat. I couldn't believe that
Hobo the greeter, the friend maker, and the PR cat had
passed away. When Brian and I had first gone in there a
year or so ago when we were visiting, Hobo came right up
to us and purred and made us feel welcome. We especially
liked him because we had a cat named Snookums that
looked so much like him, same markings, same

friendliness. We had picked up Snookums when we lived in the Ogden Canyon called Eden, Utah. He was a stray. When we moved to California we took him in the van with us. He was in a carrier and he howled and groaned all the way there, like he was being killed. He hated cars. After a few years of spoiling him, he got up to eighteen pounds. Then Brian decided that we were going to move back to Hawaii.

Our stopping off place was at his brother David's condo on Maui in the town of Kihei and he is allergic to cats so I had to find a decent home for Snookums back in Auburn, California. I did find one, but then after almost a year, the owner got another cat. Snookums took umbrage at that and disappeared. He felt that he had to be King or he's outta here!

I, at the time, did not know of his disappearance but one day my daughter called me to tell me that she had seen Snookums in her back yard. We had lived for a time at her house with Snookums just before we went to Hawaii. My daughter lived fifteen miles away from Snookum's new owner and it had been snowing. He had traveled all that way back to find me. Sniff Sniff. The new owner said that he would come back and eat sometimes, as she would leave food in the back yard for him but never came in again. He was mad at her. That's why we loved to see Hobo and now he is gone, too.

HOBO, BOOK STORE CAT
May 2003 – Jan. 2014

Dear friends, it is with heavy hearts that we inform you, if you did not already know, that we had to say goodbye to our sweet boy, Hobo, on Friday, Jan. 17th. We thank you all so much for your generous help with Hobo's vet bills, as we struggled to find out what was making him so sick. Despite our hopes, it was confirmed that Hobo did, indeed, have a "mass" nested in his thoracic cavity, pressing against both his heart, and his esophagus and trachea. We kept him as comfortable as possible, but finally it just got too difficult for him to do even the most basic things, and it was time to let him go.

All pets are special. This is obvious to anyone who has ever owned a pet, and to many people who have never had the chance, but who still love animals. Both Kevin and Kasey have owned many pets, as have most of you -- yet we all recognized that Hobo was an extra special guy. He was, in many ways, the community's cat. He belonged to everyone who came to the bookstore, who found us on facebook, who read Hobo's book, who had Hobo visit their library or school. He was a real gem, and he touched all of us with his gentle nature, his goofy antics, his affectionate attitude.

more regularly, until he was a full-time member of the staff at From My Shelf, from 2010 to 2014.

Hobo's jobs at the bookstore included playing with children, delighting crazy cat people, rearranging sidelines, regular maintenance on computers and the cash register, checking air flow of heating vents, and soaking up sunshine to spread to everyone he met. Hobo was also a regular model for photographs, as well as being the icon for a wooden sidewalk statue (by carver Bill Schlegel), a Christmas ornament (by Mary Wise), local children's artwork, and for the weekly Gazette newspaper column, "Cat Tales: Writing

Hobo spent most of his
e working in customer
rvice. His first job was at
2vin's gym, Touch of Well-
ss, where Hobo first ad-
oted Kevin in the summer
2003. In the beginning,
obo worked outside as a
eeter, then inside, check-
g on all aspects of gym
e. After the gym closed,
obo took some time off
find himself, as writ-
s are wont to do. After
uch quiet reflection and
ew AWOL adventures
eaking out screened-in
ndows to go for a sum-
er moonlight stroll or
o), Hobo began work on
s memoir, a children's
ok entitled, Hobo Finds
Home. This was excit-
g, but Hobo once again
arned to be with the pub-
He felt customer service
is his calling, and the
okstore was the answer.
began coming to From
/ Shelf, first only spo-
lically for book signings
d children's events, then
about Reading."

Hobo is not only sur-
vived by the humans he
lived with, Kevin Coolidge
and Kasey Cox, but by two
girl cats, Gypsy and Velvet;
all the people who have
worked at From My Shelf
as staff members, but especially Jen, Rachel, and Kris;
regular bookstore visitors,
both locals and tourists
alike; and a community of
people, near and far, who
thought of Hobo as their
special cat, too. Thanks for
sharing him with us.

We'd like to thank Dr.
Haas, and all the people
who work at the Wellsboro
Small Animal Hospital for
the incredible kindness and
patience they showed us
during Hobo's illness. We'd
also like to thank everyone
who donated to Hobo's
fundraiser. After paying Hobo's bills, the remainder of
the monies raised from our
fundraiser will be donated
to the Animal Care Sanctu-
ary here in Wellsboro.

February 1, 2014

Today Brian and I got up and lounged around and then decided to go to see the famous Pennsylvania Grand Canyon. People from all over come to ride their bicycles along the river that is at the bottom of the canyon. Well it's only ten miles from here but we still couldn't find it. I'm sure that later in this book I will have found it and will include some pictures of it.

I went to the local Community Center and met some nice people there. Of course I got on to the subject of what I am doing in this little town. The inhabitants of this town show such pride and love for it that all of my connections are usually very informed and interested in the subject.

I met a very nice woman there named Shirley Alexander nee Heatwole and she knows about her history here. She also wants to take me one day soon to our Grand Canyon. She said that there is a real cute little community town there. I am more interested in seeing the town than I am in seeing the canyon.

When Brian was here visiting he likes to take walks and I don't walk that far. Yesterday he walked up town and went into a little shop called "The Pop Culture Shop". I had seen it before but never really knew what they did there. What brought him to go in there was that they had a sandwich board out in front of it that said that they play games in there together, one being MahJong. He knew that I like MahJong so he went in there and used their phone to call me (he left his here) and invite me to Tuesday at 10 AM and Saturdays at noon for MahJong. Brian said that there were people in there playing and yelling and having a lot of fun. Then on Fridays I go to the Ladies Club at 11 AM and then we go to lunch.

Anja (pronounced Anya) owner of the Pop Culture Shoppe and me

Once per month I go to the Mansfield to the Civil War Round Table meetings in the evening. Oh, I am forgetting that on the 13th of February I go to the Writer's meeting. I am going to be a busy woman if I can keep up with all of this. I am leaving out the Thursday night Trivia Night at the Timeless Restaurant. I was invited to join a group of ladies to join them at their table to play. This will all be fodder material for my book.

While Brian is here, we've been invited to dinner at Celia's home. We have never met her husband and I am looking forward to that little get together tonight.

February 2, 2014
9:30 AM

Last night we went to dinner as planned at Celia's home and met her husband, Steve. They are such a nice and friendly couple. The food was delicious. She made a roast that fell apart, baked potatoes, corn, broccoli and salad. We arrived at 4:30 PM and left at 7:30 PM. Brian goes to bed at 8PM and I like to stay up until midnight so it's kind of difficult but I still like it better when he is here.

I was dreading this morning to come because Brian was going to be heading out to Bethlehem, Pennsylvania, where his office is which is 185 miles. There was to be a meeting at 1:30:PM. I get this same sinking feeling when he is on the road...so I got up early and washed and dried his clothes and he packed up and we were sitting here talking about his leaving time and he said that he was going to wait for another forty-five minutes. While waiting, his phone let him know that a message came in and it was his boss saying that they were having a snowstorm and the meeting was cancelled. We had just noticed that there were little flakes coming down here so the only bad part is if it's coming this way, tomorrow it will be over here and he'll have to drive in it. I'm so sick of worrying all the time but that's me and I can't seem to help it.

Sometimes I think that I am bragging too much about this little town and then I came across this on Amazon.com: there's a Kindle book called "A Walking Tour Of Wellsboro, Pennsylvania" by Doug Gelbert.

This is what I found in one of the paragraphs: *"The Wellsboro Historic District was listed on the National Register of*

Historic Places in 2005. The architecture of the district reflects the level of maturity in Wellsboro at the turn of the twentieth century, by which time many of the resources in the district were in place. High-style houses were built for civic and industrial leaders, primarily along Main Street and West Avenue. A feature which adds considerably to the visual character of the district is found along portions of both Main Street and Central Avenue, which have boulevards with trees, grass, and Wellsboro's signature gas street lights mounted on cast iron poles."

I am so proud of being a part of this little burg and also the fact that my family is part of its history.

Natural Ways
February 4, 2014

When Brian is here he goes to bed about 8PM at the latest. The TV is in the bedroom so I have to watch it with the captions on and down real low…so I go to bed about 9:30PM or so. That means that I wake up at about four or five in the morning. So here I am looking for sites on the computer for Sofield stuff.

After Brian left and I shed a tear or two, I got this creepy feeling that this is probably about the same place where my great-grandma stood and said good-bye for the last time to her husband as he went off to war. I know that I am being melodramatic but this is a book that includes many of my thoughts and feelings and those were the thoughts.

We are having very increment weather this winter and driving in this weather is not for sissies. Brian is night blind and has appointments that take him more than

172 | Audrey Sofield Barber

twenty miles from where he is staying and sometimes at night. His pupils don't dilate like most people's do, so at night they don't get larger to let light in. When I first started going out with him one night we were in the bay area of Northern California on the freeway at night and it was raining. He looked over at me and said, "If you knew how much I couldn't see, you'd get out of the car!" That's what I worry about when he leaves. His eyes are light blue and all you can see is that little black dot in the middle, day or night. He tries to make his appointments in the daytime but that isn't always possible.

I knew that as soon as he left this morning that I was going to have to go and meet people and get cheered up, so I decided that I'd go to that little store with games and see what I could do. It's called "Pop Culture Shoppe." It's right around the corner from the Book Store on East Ave. When I went in I was greeted by the owners, Anja (with a short A and silent J) and Julian, her husband, very nice and friendly people. They have oodles of games for people of all ages and they send stuff all over the world. I forgot to take pictures today but I will. They were playing American Mahjong and I play the Chinese version. They said that they know of a lady that plays that kind and they are going to give her my phone number and I'll be there with bells on. It's not an easy game to learn to play…and then you're hooked!

NATURAL WAYS on Crafton Street, Toni Smith, owner

After that I was going to go to the grocery store but I remembered that there was a little shop that Brian also had found in one of his walks. He always has his eyes out for the little Mom and Pop shops and he came home the other day with some eggs from free roaming chickens as that is the only kind that I will eat. It was from a little store at 17 ½ Crafton Street.

He suggested that I go over there and look around….so I went. It turned out to be a consignment shop. It features Natural Herbs and spices, and…..well I'll just show you some pictures. The lady that owns it is Toni Smith. She is pretty young and very friendly. (Have I mentioned that I love this town?). In fact after talking to her for a while we both decided that we are going to go to my landlady's buffet next Sunday in Mansfield. So I have that to look forward to next Sunday. Here is what the inside of her little place looks like.

Some of her nice inventory
(See page 352 for what her store looks like with full inventory!)

The Community Center
February 7 and 8, 2014

I don't know what is happening to me but I'm pretty sure that I am losing it. Last week when I went to the Community Center, better known as the Senior Center but we seniors don't want to call it that, I met everyone, had lunch there and signed up to wrap food packages for the Meals-on-Wheels program on Wednesdays and Fridays. Well last Wednesday I didn't go because Brian had come to visit for a few days. I called and let them know. Then along came Friday and I enjoy going across the street to the Ladies Friday meetings, so I realized that I had made two appointments at the same time. Then yesterday Mr. Cunningham from Cunningham Surveyors returned a call that I had made to him a few days before. I wanted to hire him to take the deeds from my ancestors and let me know where they all lived. I had the deeds here at the house but I needed them to be identified as to exactly where the properties are now and who lives in them. I plan on going to their homes and pay a little visit and inform them who used to own it.

Well, Mr. Cunningham and I spoke for a while and I liked his knowledge of the area and his down-to-earth personality, so I made an appointment with him to bring my deeds over to his office. When did I make the appointment you ask? Well, I, of course, made it at 11:AM Friday. It didn't dawn on me until yesterday (Friday) morning what I had done. I had made three, yes, three appointments on the same day at the same time, so here is what I did. I called the Senior Center at 8:30AM, before they opened, of course, ahem, and told them that I was so sorry but that my memory seems to have vanished and that I wouldn't be coming there on Fridays. I now hesitate to make commitments that are further ahead than, oh say, one day. I promise you that I will go and face the music at the Senior Center soon. I'll endeavor to go next Wednesday. I know that I am coming across selfish but for the sake of my good conscience, I will continue to rationalize and here is the rationalization to follow: these Friday Ladies meetings are very interesting and you learn a lot about different things there. Each week an assignment is given to one lady to cover a bio about different people in history. I am not sure if you choose who you want to pick or if they pick them for you. Last week it was done on the von Trapp Family. It really was interesting. They have a table that has presentation materials on it, including pictures and other displays. Then yesterday (yes, I went there instead of going to wrap food packages (Just leave me alone!), it was on the Tiffany family. They usually start with the earliest patriarch or matriarch of the beginnings of the business and show the evolution of it as time progresses. As was with the von Trapps, they were all singers almost from babyhood.

The Tiffany Family evolved from a man named Comfort Tiffany and down to his son, Lewis, and his love for anything colorful and sparkly as a child, up to what we have today at Tiffanys.

Anyway I digressed as usual.

That Ladies' meeting starts at 11AM and the food wrapping at the Senior Center starts at about the same time. Oh, how I hated to call those people to tell them that I am using another excuse for not being there. I'm going to use my excuse, to myself of course, that I want to enjoy my twilight years in this little gas-lighted town doing the things that I have never gotten to do before...or should I say, "never have availed myself to doing before."

These ladies that I see at the meetings and the men that I see at the Civil War Round Table and the group that I will be seeing at the 'writers round table" meeting that I plan on going to once per month, wake up my mind to learning about the world around me...the nice things, not the horrible things that seem to be going on now, but cultural things. It seems that all you see in the news today (and probably yesterday, too) is who killed whom, et cetera. This is not to mention all the news that you really don't see on TV but on certain computer stations that lead one to believe that we are all doomed. Maybe we are, but I think that I would rather concentrate on biographies and culture. I know what you are thinking, "you are 80 years old and you are now just getting around to this way of thinking?" and yes, you are right, it's true.

As I think back on my life I have never been exposed to or had the desire to get involved in these pursuits. My parents were musicians, entertainers. All I knew, when growing up in Riverside, California, was music. I can't remember a time when our doorbell would ring when my parents had company and that company didn't have their musical instruments with them. Then I got married at eighteen, had five children by the time I was thirty with plenty of marriage problems. Then after twenty-nine years of marriage, got a divorce and remarried three years later to my husband, Brian, until now. He is younger that I am but I have learned a lot from him and have gotten to travel (within the US) and lived in a lot of places that I wouldn't have gotten to even see, had I not met him. Since I've been with him, I've lived in different towns in California, Utah, Hawaii (two different islands) and now Pennsylvania.

Brian is more educated than I. I didn't go to college although I did graduate from high school by the skin of my teeth, whereas Brian graduated from college and for most of his adult life has been self-educated by reading and studying world affairs, science astrology and basically anything he can get his hands on. There is such a difference between the two of us it's magic why we are still together and we have been together for about thirty-two years. Looking back, I have no idea how much education my parents had. I don't even know if they finished high school. They were born in the mid-1890s and school didn't seem as important back then as it has been from the mid-1900s until now.

In all the pictures of my parents that I have gleaned, it shows them with their violins in their hands from their youth on up. They both *seemed* educated enough, I mean they could read and write and hold a decent conversation but from that point on, I don't know. My mother had beautiful handwriting and she said that in her younger days she had been hired by greeting card companies to write out their card entries. I think that my parents would have loved Wellsboro because as small as it is, there is so much going on in the way of entertainment. All towns and cities have entertainment but you usually have to get in the car and drive for miles to get to it. Here they have an entertainment center right on Main Street where there is usually some event happening much of the time. I so love it here.

This morning, I received my usual phone call from Brian with a "good morning" salutation and he asked me what I was going to do today and I didn't know as yet. Since it is supposed to snow again tomorrow I wanted to get out and do something today. No sooner did he ask me that and I got a phone call from Celia asking me to meet her for lunch in town and then she will come over to my house for a game of Upword. Upword is a form of Scrabble only you build words on top of the tiles. I love Upword <u>and</u> Celia, so that is my plan for today. I'll get back to you tonight.

It's now almost 5PM and I had a very nice time with Celia. I walked, yes, you heard me right, walked to the Harlands Restaurant in the cold. It's three blocks from here. I took pictures of myself but they showed too many wrinkles so I am not sharing them. Selfies as they call them are not for old people…not enough distance. I wish I knew how do Photoshop. Anyway, we had a nice lunch and then we both came over to my place and we played

Upword for about 2 ½ hours. Please don't ask me who won, ok? So I will bid you all good evening for now and we'll see what tomorrow brings.

My Plan
February 11

I want to tell you what my plan is. If you recall I made an appointment with Mr. Cunningham, the surveyor. I left many copies of deeds with him concerning the part that Ezkiel Jones played in the establishment of Wellsboro. Then I left another deed that I feel is a link between my great-grandmother Helen Jones Sofield and the Ezekiel Jones that was a blacksmith here in 1810-1815.

From what I have figured out on my own, which isn't too reliable, that house on the corner of King and Main Street on the east side of King is one of the properties that Jones purchased from the township to help start Wellsboro. He was the blacksmith. One of the things that makes this so interesting is that, that is the house that everyone in town talks about as having the red front door gifted to the owners of the house back then by Mary Todd Lincoln. I am anxious to talk to the present owners about that and to tell them about what my past history with that house may be.

As for my direct relationship with the Sofields that I have talked about, that can be technically followed right back and proven. As for the Ezekiel Jones relationship, so far, I am only surmising because there is a missing link.

That link is the one between my great-grandmother and Ezekiel. All I have to go by are her age and last name compared with when Ezekiel Jones came here. It doesn't give his age but I am assuming that he wasn't a very old man because he is mentioned in 1810 and again when he sold some property to a Sofield in 1848. That date is the last date that he is mentioned in a deed or any book that I have read. In 1850 my great-grandmother was nineteen and living with a group of people, one of who was the man, Joseph Sofield, who bought the parcel/house from Jones.

I have been practicing how to approach the people who live in that house. I believe he is a dentist. In my head I am standing at his door with my paperwork in my hand and I knock. It is very cold outside and I am wondering how I am going to ask if I can come in. I have practiced and practiced and it's very hard to know what to say while standing on their cold porch. My paperwork should be done in a week or so, so I will hope that by then I will have come up with something clever.

Today I went to play Mahjong at the Pop Culture shop and I just don't feel like I am ever going to learn to play that game the American Way. I have always played the Chinese version and they are very different. The ladies were very patient with me but I just don't think that I will ever learn to play it this way.

Later that night I got my massage and it seemed very relaxing but somehow in the middle of the night I started having my old problems back with my sciatica. Plus I am also allergic to showering or bathing in water with chorine in it and now that I have been doing that since living here it caught up with me last night in bed where it feels like I'm being stuck with little needles and it itches. Now I'll have to buy a showerhead that's filtered.

The next morning, I didn't feel so good as I couldn't sleep and kept itching. I did find something interesting today though. I went to Joyce Tyce's web site about Wellsboro and found the following paragraph: *"Also from Lola W. Franke, the following on early settlers buried here: from History of Tioga County, 1897, On the corner where Dr. Shearer now lives, Ezekiel Jones had a house and blacksmith shop. On the corner, across the street from his place, was a small house in which lived Col. Field, father of Prescott Field. Joshua Emer's reminiscences. "*

Civil War Round Table, Redux
February 12

This evening I went to the Civil War Round Table again. Roger Wagner came and picked me up and it was very interesting because it happened to be Lincoln's Birthday and the whole round table said very interesting things about him. I had heard of most of the stories but there were opinions of him also. I'm not sure if any of you have heard that opinion of him that he may have been homosexual.

He slept with Joshua Speed for a few years when he first arrived at Springfield, Illinois. This was a common practice of the day. He showed up broke and broken and Joshua Speed offered to let him stay with him and that ended up to be a few years. Since they slept in the same bed all those years it is assumed to people in today's culture that they were more than just friends. Whether they were gay or not, which I just find hard to grasp, it doesn't change the fact that he was a wonderful, compassionate leader not to mention, humble, conscientious, humorous and physically strong.

People that had hated his politics also made them hate him, the man, until they would go and actually meet him. Then they would come out saying that he was Christ-like. When the soldiers would go AWOL and get caught it was up to him to decide what to do with them and nine times out of ten he would say, "If it were me, I would probably have done the same thing" and he would let them live.

I don't really know what kind of a man my great-grandfather, Alfred, was but I have picked up some clues along the way and I have shared them with you. One thing, though, that made me feel good about him is that the Emancipation Proclamation was announced mid 1862 that beginning on January 1, 1863, slaves belonging to the plantation owners of the seceding states would be emancipated and they were welcome to join in with the fight. There were many prejudice Union Soldiers that walked off from fighting as they said that they weren't going to fight for freedom of the Ni—ers. My great-grandfather stayed and wasn't killed until six months after the proclamation was in place.

I read from Joyce Tice's website about a true story that was told about an event here in Wellsboro back in the slave days. There were two young runaway slaves that ended up here in Wellsboro. They were both boys and the local judge at the time hired them to do some work for him…it appeared that he knew that they were runaway slaves. If I remember correctly, there were some rednecks that found out about it and tried to turn them in so that they could collect their ransom money (great constitution that we had) but some local boys didn't want that to happen so they tricked these rednecks and the runaways got away. It's so odd that nothing really changes…there are those nowadays that would fit right into those two categories. I'm just glad that I am in the nice group.

Letters to the Editor
February 13

My kids always call me Lucy, after *I Love Lucy* because I guess I get myself in some Lucy-type situations. Well, today was one of them. I am going to take a chance and hope that it isn't one of the things where "you have to be there" to see how funny it is. I went to town to get my nails done and there are only two nail places in this town and one of them doesn't do fills like I have done. Two doors down there is the second nail place.

Let me describe the layout of this salon. You walk in and right in front of the door is a little standing room in front of the counter. To my right was the beautician and she was working on a lady's hair. Then right across the counter was another lady sitting in a chair. We all started talking and they asked me what brought me to Wellsboro and I gladly

Help needed—

To the editor:

I have recently moved here to Wellsboro to write a book about my last four generations, three of whom were born and raised here. I go clear back to 1815 and concentrate on the 1850s and 1860s. My great grandfather was Alfred Sofield. He was Justice of the Peace here at that time and joined the call from Lincoln, became a recruiter and was killed on July 1, 1863, at Gettysburg as a Bucktail.

I am writing a book based on things that I have found from the County Recorder's Office and Scott Gitchell at the Historical Society. If any of you that know a lot about the history of this wonderful, quaint little town that includes any of the Sofields or Jones, please give me a call at 808-346-7549 or email me at audrey@wellsbororoots.com Also check on Facebook at wellsbororoots by Audrey Sofield Barber

AUDREY SOFIELD/BARBER Wellsboro

told them about my ancestry quest and how I loved this adorable little town. Then they started asking me all these questions and we were all laughing and talking to each other and finally the lady getting her hair done got up and she and I stood there talking for a bit and then I looked over at the chair where she had been sitting while having her hair done and the beautician started doing another lady's hair. I looked closer at the new lady getting her hair done and I said to her, "You look familiar, do I know you?" She answered, "Well you've known me now for about 20 minutes from when I was sitting in the chair talking to you from across the counter. Everyone started

Disappointed—

To the editor:

I am writing to you to express my extreme discontentment in your choice to include an obituary for a cat in the Jan. 29 edition.

What a blatant display of disrespect toward every member of the families who share an obituary on the same page. A family lost a child of two years, one a veteran of the United States Navy, along with several others. All of these losses share the same page with the death of a feline.

Can you imagine the hurt of the mother who opened the paper to see her baby daughter s obituary next to a cat? You have made a mockery of yourselves and your paper. There are members of the community that have done a lifetime of good who should be remembered and respected here, and instead you ve made them a joke.

I am surprised and disappointed in the lack of respect that you have shown these families. What a shame.

KARI MASCHO
Westfield

cracking up. I wish you had all been there because it really was funny when it happened.

Tonight I am supposed to go to the writer's class at the book store but it has been snowing so hard that I don't know if they are going to go ahead with it or not. So I called. I'm glad that I called because it had to be cancelled. Darn. I was so looking forward to that. I'll have my book written before I get to attend it.

Well, here is something that I think is pretty interesting. I'm sure that you will all have an opinion about this, even some of you that won't agree with my opinion…but, oh, well, here goes.

Maybe I am a Pollyanna because I have been accused of having my head in a pink cloud before, but my pink cloud, in my mind, was represented in this little town. I know that I was overthinking the innocence that Wellsboro seemed to represent to me, but in the above newspaper article it kind of brought me back down to earth again and made me realize that there still are all kinds of people living here and not everyone will be on the same page.

When I first read that kitty obituary it warmed my heart. Certainly not because Hobo had died but because it brought home the community closeness that I, after having only lived here for a little over a month, have come to experience.

I realize that everyone has different viewpoints on different situations but here is mine regarding the kitty obituary. To me, if I am feeling a little down, if I see even a picture or video of a cat I can feel that depressed feeling start to ebb. When I would go in that bookstore where Hobo lived with his family I would always look for him. He looked so much like my Snookums that we used to have. I feel that the people at the book store knew the closeness that a lot of people that went in there, had with Hobo and it was kind of a tribute to him for bringing so much comfort and joy to so many people. To some people, their animals are much like their own children, to a point, of course.

I think that another reason that this obituary was appropriate is because it was the storeowners' way of thanking the friends who gave money to help try to save his life. I feel very sad that there was a little girl's obituary on that page, not because it was shared by Hobo but because now her parents' lives will be changed forever and I would think that the parents of this child would have more to be concerned with than to be insulted by Hobo's presence.

My Day in Church

February 16

Here it was Sunday and it's *still* snowing. It's beautiful but even I can get cabin fever now and then. When it snows on Sundays this little burg goes to sleep...unless you are a churchgoer. I'm not...but it's right across the street and I went once before and I like meeting new people.

I went to the Internet to see what was going to be their topic and it looked interesting. There were going to be two Lutheran ladies, one a pastor, and the other her assistant. They came over here from Gambia, Africa, just to share with this Presbyterian Church group their experiences with being Christian in a 95% Muslim Country. Now that did sound interesting. The next thing that I read was it was to be followed by a potluck lunch down in the cafeteria. Then I had no doubts, I was going to go to church!

This is the same church that Roger Wagner (Civil War Round Table man) and his wife go to so I would at least know someone. I went in and got dressed, even put make-up on and walked, you guessed it, across the street to the church. As I sat there I was admiring the beautiful interior and most of all the stained glass huge windows.

The service started and the pastor welcomed people there and talked a little about different things that they were doing. He then introduced the two ladies from Gambia. They had on their pretty colorful attire from Africa and the main lady pastor, Reverend Fatima Thomas, and her colleague Neema Lugaisa. I was very anxious to hear about their experiences in West Africa…especially regarding the Muslims.

You hear so much talk over here, much of it, I feel, is propaganda. I wanted to hear for myself what really goes on. Much to my dismay, I couldn't understand a thing that she said. I really mean "a thing." What really troubled me, though, is that when she said something that was obviously funny, the whole congregation would laugh…so once again, it was me. I really struggled to understand her.

Then the choir got up and sang an African Song with bongos and it was great! I'd love to have a CD on that.

When it was over we went downstairs to the very large cafeteria and had a feast. Everything was great. I sat with a nice couple and told them why I was there and we laughed and talked for a while. Then the local pastor, Pastor Glen Hellead, had the ladies from Africa get up and accept a gift of $1450.

To the left is a photograph of the pastor and his really cute wife. After they accepted their gift the one lady, Pastor Thomas, was wiping her eyes and getting a little teary from having to leave and accepting the gift. I then went up and asked the pastor to take my picture with the two ladies.

He admitted that he had never used an iPad before. Here we were posing and he kept trying to press the right button until it clicks.

The pastor kept saying, "It won't click."

"It should be working," I said.

Finally, after quite some time, he said, "There, it clicked!"

On the next page is what I found when I took the iPad back.

It seems that mine aren't the only ears that aren't quite working very well. I kept turning the pages of the pictures and I thought that they would never end. He took eighteen pictures! Another thing that caught my eye was that the lady on the left of me was always smiling…even when we weren't taking pictures...she was really cute. Then the lady on my right…she was another story. If you look at each of the pictures, she barely moved an eyelash. She looked like a wax statue in these pictures.

Then I went over to the table and started doing a little cleaning and folding the tablecloths when a couple approached me. They introduced themselves and seemed to know why I was in Wellsboro.

When this couple introduced themselves to me, she told me that her maiden name was Bache. That really got my attention because over at the Historical Society, Scott Gitchell told me that he learned somehow that after my great-grandpa was killed that one of the Baches had somehow gotten the twisted saber or sword off AJS's body and brought it home to give to my great-grandmother. I also have a deed from Joseph Sofield (who I believe was my great-grand-uncle) to William Bache Jr.

It feels like a lot of the friends that they had back then are in the same group of friends that socialize now. It's a very strange feeling that is very hard to explain. It's a cohesive feeling with the past. This couple is a delight and super friendly. I'd love to be able to get together with them sometime and go over all they know and vice versa.

It's been a good day.

One Step Forward and One Step Backward
February 17-20

It started out so great. I was calling people with the same last names as some of the soldiers' last names in AJS's unit and company. It was going good and I was getting some real steps ahead. As I have said before, this little town—and really the whole of Tioga County—is into its own history more than I have ever been acquainted with before...and with that said, I was getting some good responses.

Everyone I talked to had a relative with papers that they had collected showing their Wellsboro family history. I found the great-great grandson of Benjamin H. Warriner. He was one of the four captains in the 149th Company A unit. Wow, I got a real connection going.

As I was leaving to go to my Thursday night Trivia Night my phone rang. I answered it and a lady on the other end said that she was told by her grandfather that I had called looking for an ancestor of Jesse and Alfred Borden. The girl on the phone was a Borden and I told her the two names of the men that she should be looking for. She said that she remembered that there were some relatives that had gone into the Civil War from here and she was almost certain that these were them. I didn't have a lot of time to talk to her and I am going to call her back tonight.

Wow! Two connections in one day. First Tom Warriner and now Denise (Borden). Now I have gotten Chief of Police Bodine (pronounced here with a long I) Pam Shipe, relative of many of the pioneers that were here in the beginning and now the direct ancestor of the Baches. I have gotten permission to have my picture taken with them. I'd like to have a group picture.

Those were the steps forward.

What follows are the steps backward.

I got a brainstorm to go to the original, handwritten census of the 1850s and 1860s so that once and for all, I could get an exact parcel where my relatives lived. I was of the mistaken idea that the census takers went from door to door in a regular fashion and I would look down the line and see who lived next door to whom and take it over to Scott at the Historical Society and show it to him and that he could identify certain home owners and that would pinpoint where my family lived. WRONG!!!

I can't figure out why these census takers went in the path that they did but here is what they did, for instance. They would do one house on Pearl Street, then what would look like on the census would be "next door" to that home, would actually be back up to Water Street, two blocks away, then a couple of them back on Main Street and so forth. I was so disappointed.

On the other hand, though, I learned so much from Scott. He has the most reflective memory that I have ever encountered. I mentioned the name of Bache to him and he, off the top of his head, recited their genealogy starting in the early 1800s and brought it up to today. He is no relation to them. He gave me the history of the property that is on the corner of King and Main, you know, the one with the red door that I feel was first purchased by Ezekiel L. Jones

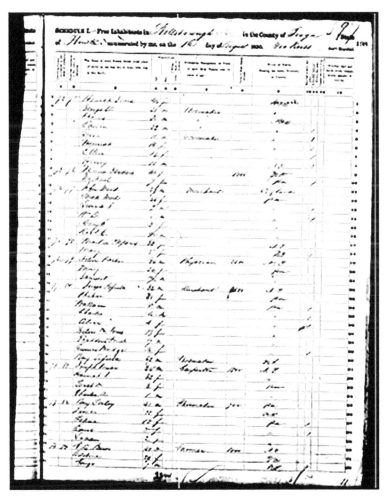

and who may be my great-great-grandfather? It seems that according to history, that Scott is very familiar with; it had been purchased by Hannah Shearer back in 1862.

Mrs. Shearer had been a very close friend of Mary Todd Lincoln to the point where the Shearers had even gone to visit the Lincolns at the White House before they moved to Wellsboro. Mr. Shearer had a lung condition so he visited Wellsboro and felt that this fresh air here would be the healthy way to go so they moved here. They stayed in a hotel while waiting to settle in their home. I have yet to prove beyond a shadow of doubt that Ezekiel L. Jones, who was the first Wellsborian resident to purchase the property that the Shearers ended up owning and living in. I just have circumstantial reasons to think (and hope) that my great-grandmother Helen Jones Sofield was his daughter. The ages would be close to make it possible but I am missing that one link that would put them together.

Jones was first purchasing property in Del Mar, which is just about ten miles from Wellsboro. Next he is purchasing property here on Main and King, among other properties close by. I find no other Jones' living here at that time. This took place in and between 1810-1815. He had the blacksmith shop where the Shearers owned later and Dr. Black owns today. Then it shows that between 1836-1844 he was doing real estate transactions with Joseph Sofield. Moving up to 1850 census has my great-grandmother Helen M. Jones living with Joseph Sofield and others at the age of nineteen. Too bad that it doesn't say where the house was but back then there were only a few blocks of residential homes.

I feel that I am so close but just can't get a full take on it. When I get one step forward and then have to step back a pace or two it's so frustrating. I am hoping that when the surveyor gets through with my deeds, et cetera, that then there will be more light shed on it.

I went to the Friday morning Ladies Club at 11AM and it was quite interesting. It was about three generations of artists, one of them being Andrew Wyeth. The presenter did a slide presentation.

I loved his style of painting and her delivery was very well put. Then we all went to lunch at Endless Destinations. After that I came home for a time and then it was such a nice day out compared to what it has been I walked over to the Police Station that is three blocks from here so that I could see and meet Chief of Police Bodine. I was equipped with my Ipad camera so that we could have our picture taken together if we found out that his Bodines were the same lineage as Lewis Bodine that was the captain that took my great-grandpas place when he was killed. He wasn't there at first but in another building down the street so I went down the street and he was in a meeting. I thought that I would go across that street to visit my friend Toni, who owns the cute little store that specialized in anything organic or natural.

I stayed at the store for about half an hour, purchased a couple of things and then my phone rang. I had left my card with Mr. Bodine's receptionist and he was calling to tell me that he was out of the meeting now. I was so anxious to get over there and meet him so I practically ran over there. I was so surprised to see how young he was, or at least looked. After showing him the list of soldiers under my great-grandfather he called his mother in Florida who has the family history clear back to before the Revolutionary War and she wasn't familiar with Lewis Bodine but she would do some more research.

I came home without taking a picture (mainly because there wasn't a third party there to take it) and got onto Ancestry.com and found Lewis Bodine living here in Wellsboro when he was ten years old in 1840, which does make him the right age to have fought in the Civil War…but it doesn't show him here after that!

Phooey!

Is this another step back?

A Play and Church
February 22

Saturday night and what shall I do? I usually just write on my book or watch TV or read, but yesterday I had picked up a brochure to a stage play and I thought that maybe I'd go for it. It's usually not so much fun to go to places like that alone but I just felt like going. The weather had "warmed up" somewhat and so I looked at the address of where this play was going to take place. I really don't think that you are going to believe me when I say this, but, yes, it was down one block and across the street.

I had walked to town yesterday and went into a cute little dress shop that I hadn't noticed before. They have real trendy clothes in there, clothes that are flowey, breezy clothes, much like the 1960s attire. I know that I am going to be eighty-one in a week from today but I still wanted to be flowey!

This is the dress I bought.

Got dressed up and walked out the door at 7PM which would give me time to get a good seat. The show didn't start until 7:30PM. I grabbed a seat right in the front row. The stage was only about ten feet from the front row and only about one foot high and little by little that little place was packed to the brim.

I was so glad that I got in front. There were two teen-age girls sitting next to me that seemed to know some of the actors in the play. The actors were all in their twenties it seemed. The play was called *The End* and was basically about how different each person's take on why we are here, what it all means and how will it end.

The husband had survived Twin Towers attack on 9/11, had been a businessman and since the attack, he was suffering depression. His wife was a "Rapture" person to the extreme and was followed around the house by a Jesus person—or should I say a man in a white robe and black beard dressed like Jesus (no one saw him but her); a teen-age, smart-mouth, atheist daughter; and a young, teen-age boy who was obsessed with her.

The daughter was interested in evolution and science and would have talks with Stephen Hawking. He would be wheeling in to where she was sitting and try to tell her about why she should believe in science because it is proven. When the actor would talk like Stephen Hawking he would get a laugh. Sorry, but true.

But here was the biggest laugh of the night. There was a funny quip made in the play and one of the men in the audience way in the back laughed so loud that he made a snort. The audience couldn't quit laughing...and especially the two girls next to me. All three of us couldn't stop. The one girl kept laughing and laughing and you could tell she was trying to stop but her shoulders kept shaking up and down. We all know how that feels. The more you try to quit the harder you laugh.

When the play was over I walked outside into a beautiful clear and a little breezy night and started on my little block-and-a-half walk home and church bells gave a couple little chimes as it was probably something-thirty in the PM. There are church chimes at intervals all day and evening. It's wonderful. I felt like I was walking in a storybook.

The feeling that I get from this town is that the town itself is trying as hard as it can to be cozy—and is succeeding. So far there is nothing that I don't like about it. I hope that I never run into anything that disappoints me. Oh yes, there was the little episode at Trivia Night, and if that's all I have to face as disappointment, I'm extremely lucky.

February 23

This Sunday morning I made up my mind that I was going to go to another church and see how many people I can meet. This will be the third one. Today will be the Methodist Church that is four blocks up Main and on the corner.

The people were all very friendly and welcoming and the Pastor is a very down-to-earth type man and is very charismatic on the pulpit. You can tell by the way he speaks that it comes straight from the heart. I, of course, have my own personal opinions on the subjects that they all preach about in each church that I have gone to—but that is not my purpose in attending these church services. I attend to meet these wonderful people who live here.

As I talk to them after the services are over and they go to a room with coffee, et cetera, they all say the same thing: they all absolutely love Wellsboro. Many of them have left for jobs, et cetera, in their lives but always came back. The place is magnetic. Oh, I am certainly running into a few people who are having little tiffs, but that is to be expected. I like the ladies on both sides of the issues so I try to keep my mouth shut. I know that's a first!

Next Sunday I have tentative plans on which church to go attend. There is a Baptist Church one block behind me but I think that I may go back to St. Paul's Episcopal Church again, as that is where my relatives went. I would like to see their archives again, this time to see if I can find Ezekiel Jones in there because that is where his daughter, Helen, was baptized. I am still assuming that that is his daughter, but if he was baptized at that church, too, that would be another good clue.

Pastor Val Rummel and wife

Wow! Another Good Day!
February 27

Today started out just like any other day except that it isn't even noon yet and good things have already happened. I went over to see Scott Gitchell to ask him a couple of questions as he seems to have a photographic memory. While I was at the Historical Society I mentioned the Bucktail Reunion that has been celebrated since 1880. Scott suggested I go to the Chamber of Commerce and ask them more about it. I would love to be a part of that reunion. I only wish that my kids and grandkids could come here and also be a part of it—but they probably can't. I also hope that my husband can come.

The manager of the Chamber of Commerce came downstairs when her secretary called up to her about why I was there. She was so pleased and took my card and told me that the Bucktails would be so happy to talk to me as they are trying to contact as many relatives as possible that descend from the 149th and the 42nd Units. I would love to help them do this. She had me write down all the info that I had so she could give it to them. I am now waiting for that phone call.

I wasn't sure how often they have this celebration but on their Facebook page the event is referred to as the *Annual* Bucktail Reunion. I thought that was a pretty good clue. While reading that Facebook page, I received my first message from a Bucktail—and here it is:

To: Audrey@Wellsbororoots.com

Hello Audrey,

My name is Matt Herring and I am working with the good folks of Wellsboro to plan our 21st Annual Bucktail Reunion in August. I would be grateful to speak with you and learn more about your family history. I am well aware of your great grandfathers Bucktail history and ironically I just recently visited his grave in Gettysburg and placed a coin of remembrance there. The Ol't Boys guide us daily in our plans for our Reunions...isn't it a special bond we all share!

Please let me know how we can talk further...I will be in Wellsboro on March 19 for a Bucktail meeting and program at the Presbyterian Church.

Regards,

Matt Herring

214 | Audrey Sofield Barber

A Mixed Bag
February 28

Wow. What a see-saw day it was yesterday. My
emotions were going haywire. I would learn something
that would disappoint me, then I would learn something
that would excite me.

The first thing that I had learned that disappointed
me was when I went over to see Scott at the Historical
Society he told me that in his photographic mind he
remembered that my great-great-grandparents, John and
Julie Sofield, the ones who are buried here in Wellsboro,
actually lived in a town called Waterbury, Pennsylvania.
Now, you may ask, "why would that disappoint you?"
Here is the reason: I had pictured that when my great-
grandfather was killed that her mother-in-law was
probably nearby to help her with her children and just for
moral support. But now it makes me sad to see, according
to MapQuest, they lived thirty-eight miles from my great-
grandmother. That's a long way on horse and buggy. I
can also see from this that Betsy Weeks was living with

them. Julia's maiden name was Weeks, so I assume that is her mother…and oh my gosh, it also just hit me that she will give me another lead on where the Weeks come from. That means I have found a great-great-grandmother. Oh wow! There is now another emotion that I hadn't even counted on.

1860 United States Federal Census

Name:	John Sofield
Age in 1860:	59
Birth Year:	abt 1801
Birthplace:	New Jersey
Home in 1860:	Cummings, Lycoming, Penr
Gender:	Male
Post Office:	Waterville

Tell me this isn't confusing!

Looks like he came back alive for a while.
It also has him born in New Jersey.

Name:	John Sofield
Birth Date:	1802
Age at Death:	58
Death Date:	14 Dec 1860
Burial Place:	Wellsboro, Tioga County, Pennsylvania, USA

Okay. Now that great-great-grandfather is kind of settled, then I start worrying all over again from my poor little freshly widowed great-grandmother and also for my newly widowed great-great-grandmother who just lost her husband. I kind of hope that she moved back over to Wellsboro and lived with her daughter-in-law.

I think that the emotions run in so many different directions that I start romanticizing the events as I picture them in my mind, only to find out that it may have happened in a completely different way.

So, here is another emotion that I just experienced…when I stopped writing this for a minute or two to go to Ancestry.com to find out when exactly my great-great-grandfather died, it showed an article in the Wellsboro Eagle. That Eagle building is the building that my great-grandmother had moved her millinery business to and as I scrolled up to the top of the newspaper article it showed the address of the Eagle. I can't believe it, but it was in the first floor of the courthouse, which is right across the street. Now my imagination is starting to go wild again. I am assuming, at this point and after talking to Scott, that she lived right next door to the Presbyterian Church and I am now visualizing her walking the block to her new office/shop. The visualizing part of writing this is the most interesting part of my writing this book. If I had to be somewhere else writing it, it wouldn't be half as interesting to me.

1PM

I just received a phone call from Matt Herring, the man who is helping to put together the Bucktail Reunion. This reunion is going to be very exciting. I am trying to get two of my daughters to come along with David Finney, the cousin whom I have never met. Remember him? I speak to him on the phone but have never met him in person.

Matt was telling me what this reunion was going to consist of and it's going to be very exciting. I will be meeting with him and some of the other people putting this together on March 19th and I can't wait.

I have mentioned quite a few times in this book how everything seems to fall into place on this quest of mine. Well, it seems, that it happens to others with the same quest. Back a few years ago when Brian worked in Chambersburg/Gettysburg, he and my daughter Leslie and I took the Sofield tour. I've mentioned it before in this book. While there, there was a man dressed in a Union Soldier's uniform. He came up to us and we all took our picture with him. As it turns out, that man was Matt Herring. Just now on the phone he told me how he happened to be there. He had been looking for Rich Kohr, the man who was our tour guide, to ask him if he knew how to get a hold of Captain Sofield's ancestor. He was starting to put together information for their next Bucktail Reunion. When he came over to Rich, and told him that he was looking to get ahold of me, Rich told him that I was the one he was looking for. Unfortunately I don't remember the situation but my point is that this quest seems to lead you around to the right places.

Mountain Home Magazine
March 6

Have you ever written a page or two and accidently erase all of it? Well I just did that and I am upset to say the least. I'll go back and pretend that this is the morning...

9AM

I have plans today. First of all, Brian is coming today for a few days. Not only that but the sun is actually shining. I never thought I'd live to see the day when I would welcome the sun this much, but when you've been housebound for a week or more because it's just too cold to even peek out, then the sun is a very welcome sight.

I remember clear back to July 2010 when I was living on Maui and a lady called me out of the blue (I may have

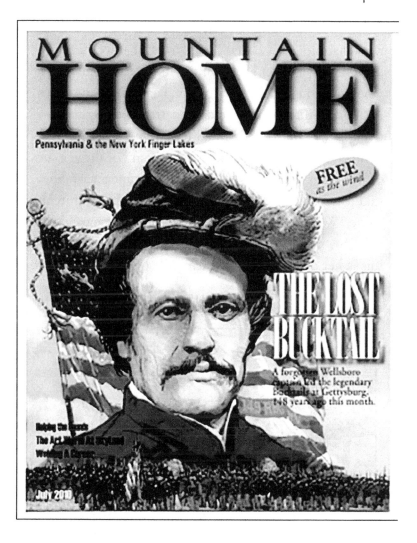

talked about this before so I will be brief) and asked me if she could write about my great-grandfather in her magazine as she was doing an article on the Bucktails and that she would feature him in it. Long story short, she did the article and the magazine cover is pictured on the previous page here.

This was in 2010 and here it is 2014 and I'm now in Wellsboro and I called the editor and asked her if I could enter another article in the June or July edition. I would like the article to include a plea for anyone reading it knowing that if they had an ancestor in either the 149th Company A Bucktail that had fought in Gettysburg to contact me. I also asked her they had any of these issues of this magazine left as I had given all mine away. She said to come on down to her office and I could purchase some. When I got there I received a very nice welcome from her and her staff. They are a very busy company and this is her office that is in the middle of them doing some repair.

Editor-in-Chief Teresa Banik Capuzzo

You can tell that she is a very busy person. To be fair, they were in the middle of doing some re-arranging but I like it when people look busy and she does look busy.

Yoda, the Mountain Home Magazine mascot

It seems to add a wonderful hominess to a business when there is a loving animal in there. This beagle was rescued by Teresa Capuzzo, the editor/owner of the magazine ten years ago—she was already eight years old when they got her. She has to wear this little diaper, as she is incontinent. She is a very sweet, little doggie.

While I was talking to Teresa, about my book, et cetera, I asked her if she knew where the old newspaper, The Agitator, used to be in the 1800s and told me that it was down on the corner of Main and Central. That location was about two blocks from where we were and if I simply looked at the top front of the building, it still had the old "Agitator" sign on the front.

I couldn't wait to get over there and take a picture of that. It is so hard to convey the emotion that I feel when something new from the past like that arises, but it certainly brings me a rush. It seems to take me back to a part of the past I feel I can almost touch. So I purchased 5 of the old magazines, thanked them and left on the run.

I drove the two blocks over there and grabbed my iPad to take a picture and I looked and looked and didn't see a thing. I went into the Bagle Shop right by where I thought it was and they told me where to go to find out so they sent me around the corner to the Deane Center which is a two story building that is a combination of offices and an entertainment center, and to ask for Pat.

I went in after inspecting the outside and finding nothing—much to my disappointment—and went to "Pat's" office and she informed me that the whole building had been the Agitator in the 1800s, but that they had done some modernizing of it and "modernized" the Agitator sign right out of the picture.

To me that was the…I will say it…*stupidest* thing they could have done. That building is, to me, like a cornerstone of the downtown, a historical monument and what do they do? They paint right over the sign. If the sign was in bad repair, it should have been salvaged in such a way that the passersby would see that it wasn't "The Agitator" any longer but would have been made aware that it used to be. I am not an artist and not even close to being one, but they could have put "Formerly The Agitator" 1868 (or whenever it was built). That really was a disappointment.

When I got home Brian was here and we walked to the diner and had a peanut butter pie. Oh, my gosh, that was so good and so bad at the same time. Then we came home and waited a bit and then went to our favorite steakhouse and ate like pigs again.

After dinner I went to the North West Savings and Loan Bank on Main Street and Crafton Street to cash a check. I really feel at home in that bank. I love Marie, the manager. I go in there every Thursday to do business and she always has a welcoming smile on her face. It's fun to do business in a bank or in other places of business when they know you by name and make you feel welcome.

Marie (my favorite banker) and me

What A Surprise!
March 9

Today is Sunday and Brian and I walked to Penn Wells Hotel for their Buffet. It was delicious—as always. After eating, we waddled back home.

I turned on the television and Brian went back out for a long walk. (He's younger than I am). I am not into long walks anymore. After my TV session I got on the computer and went to Facebook to look around and came across a Bucktail Reunion site. I told my story on the site and here is what I received back from it:

My name is Bruce Petro and I am a Civil War re-enactor with the 149th RPV as their acting Captain. I must confess when I took the field at this year's 150th reenactment at Gettysburg; I took on the persona of your ancestor Captain Sofield. I thought about him on that first day of July 1863 and the thoughts he must have had. It is truly my pleasure to contact you. I hope you would consider joining us

*in Wellsboro during the Bucktail Reunion in August. I would
treasure this encounter.
Your Most Obedient Servant,
Bruce Petro Captain 149th Bucktails Reenactment Unit*

I can't begin to tell you what it is like to have all
these pieces come together. It reminds me of a jigsaw
puzzle and similar to how one feels when they get one
more piece to fit. This message is amazing to me. I am
learning that these re-enactors take it all very seriously and
this message from him proves that they do.

I am reminded of when, in 2011, Leslie, my
daughter, Brian and I took the tour at Gettysburg and how
the tour guides would talk about Captain Sofield like they
knew him. I am so anxious now for August 1st to arrive so
that I can meet these men that have such a personal
feeling for the soldiers that they portray or talk about.

About three years or so ago I read a book that was
about how one man was a re-enactor for a Union soldier
and what his life was like. They would go out and sleep on
the ground all night for many nights in all sorts of
inclement weather. They would only eat what the soldiers
ate back then, make and drink coffee the way they had
made it back then et cetera. They are like actors in a
movie. I have never seen a re-enactment and they aren't
going to have any here at the reunion next August because
they want it to be a celebration of life not death…good
idea.

I have also found two people who are currently
writing or have just recently written a book about
Wellsboro but at this time they don't want people to know
that they are writing it…they won't even talk to me about

it. Maybe they will later. I always felt that the more people knew about your book the more people will purchase it later but I'm sure that they have their reasons.

Their book, like the one I had mentioned before, is about them being born and raised here. They wanted old pictures that dated back to the early 1920s. I am mainly interested in the years dating between 1810-1880, because, if Ezekiel Jones turns out to be my great-great-grandfather, that's when his life here in Wellsboro began.

The census for 1870 shows that my great-grandmother, Helen Sofield still lived in Wellsboro, but the 1880 census shows that she had moved to Illinois. I believe that she was waiting for my grandfather, Benjamin, to graduate from the Soldiers Orphans Home and he graduated in 1870.

Oh, oh, I just remembered that in 1878 James Sofield, her middle son, was killed in that train wreck in New York and the funeral was held on Main Street here in Wellsboro so she was still here then. Now it begins to make sense to me. She wasn't waiting for Benjamin to graduate; she had just had enough death to deal with here in Wellsboro.

If Ezekiel was her father and Mariah was her mother, they died in the1840s. That would mean her father-in-law died, then two years later her husband was killed, and four years later her mother-in-law died, and then her son James is killed. She had too many bad memories. Her Sofield relatives lived in Peoria, Illinois, and census shows that she lived with them until she got sick and moved in with her son, William, in Berkeley, California, where she died at age seventy one. She had fallen and broken her hip and I am sure that her heart was broken also. I think of her so much. I would so love to meet her and learn about her strength.

Wellsboro Walking Map
March 10

On the following page is a walking map of Wellsboro. As I looked it over, I saw the house that I am actually living in right now.

See number 13 (uh-oh is that bad luck?) Those two houses used to be one when Nathan Packer first built it in 1846 but later on it was divided into two homes. I am in one and as I look out the window I see the other one next door.

On the next few pages, you will see the walking map (and you will also be able to see that everything most certainly is "right across the street):

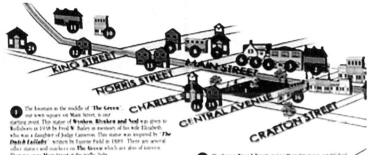

1 The fountain in the middle of "The Green", our town square on Main Street, is our starting point. This statue of **Wynken, Blynken and Nod** was given to Wellsboro in 1938 by Fred W. Bailey in memory of his wife Elizabeth, who was a daughter of Judge Cameron. This statue was inspired by "*The Dutch Lullaby*" written by Eugene Field in 1889. There are several other statues and markers on **The Green** which are also of interest. Then we cross Main Street at the traffic light.

2 The red brick building on the corner at 114 Main Street is the former Tioga County Sheriff's Residence and was constructed in 1860 at a cost of $10,000. The two-story brick structure served as the Tioga County Jail until 1985. It is now occupied by the **Tioga County Development Corporation, Wellsboro Chamber of Commerce, and Growth Resources of Wellsboro**. The elm tree in the front yard is one of the largest in existence and has been growing since sometime in the 1700's. This tree is older than Wellsboro and has been here since before the first settlers.

3 The **Tioga County Courthouse** was built in 1835. In addition to the court room and the judge's chambers, it houses the offices of many County officials.

4 Wellsboro was founded in 1806 by settlers from Delaware, Maryland and Philadelphia, it was incorporated in 1830. The town was named in honor of **Mary Wells**, wife of one of the original settlers, Benjamin Wistar Morris. **Mary Wells** (1763-1849) was a Philadelphia Quaker who came with her husband to this part of Tioga County in about 1806. This life sized bronze sculpture of **Mary Wells Morris** is located on part of the land deeded by Benjamin and Mary Wells Morris to Tioga county in 1806. Frank and Mary Hazlet of Harrisburg, PA, and Rita Bucher of Wernersville, PA, commissioned the 5'7" figure.

5 120 Main Street is the **Robinson House**, home of the Tioga County Historical Society. The building was originally a tavern operated by Alpheus Cheney, Tioga County's first Sheriff. In the early 1830's, Samuel Dickinson added four more rooms to the front of the tavern, two upstairs and two downstairs. It was later purchased by John L. Robinson. The annex at the right rear is a replica of the First National Bank of Wellsborough, of which Mr. Robinson was a founder.

6 126 Main Street, the law offices of **Walrath & Coolidge**, was the residence of the Honorable Henry W. Williams, constructed in 1883. At that time he was President Judge of Tioga County and in 1887 he was appointed to the Supreme Court of Pennsylvania.

7 The **First Presbyterian Church** at 130 Main Street was built in 1894. At that time it was hailed as the "the finest church of its size in

8 The **Green Free Library** at 134 Main Street was established in 1912 by an endowment from Charles Green of Roaring Branch. In 1936, the library moved into the beautiful house called "Chester Place" which was built by Chester Robinson, brother and business associate of John L. Robinson. The **Gmeiner Art and Cultural Center** at the right of the library was a gift to Wellsboro from the late Arthur Gmeiner of Denver, originally from the Narrows area of Tioga County.

9 140 Main Street is known as the **Lincoln Door House**. The front door of this residence (painted red in contrast to the dark green of the building) was a gift from Abraham Lincoln to Dr. and Mrs. J.B. Shearer when they bought this home in 1958. Mrs. Lincoln and Mrs. Shearer were close friends in Springfield, Illinois and the door came from a building there.

10 Located at the west end of Main Street is the oldest grocery store in Wellsboro, the **West End Market**. First opened in 1902, the store has been operated as a convenience market, a deli market, and a bulk food store. The building is now home to **The West End Market Café**.

11 Just around the corner at 10 West Avenue is the **Carleton Nursing Home**, formerly the home of Leonard Harrison, banker and businessman, who donated 121 acres of land bordering Pine Creek, and known then as "*The Lookout*" to the commonwealth in 1922. This area is now known as Leonard Harrison State Park.

12 Across the street and down a block on the corner at 141 Main Street is the **Jesse Robinson Manor** which was built in 1887 by a son of John L. Robinson. It has been described as **Queen Anne style in the true English Spirit**.

13 As you start back toward **The Green**, the second and third houses were originally one building. It was constructed circa 1840's as the residence of the **Packer** family. After the death of the Honorable Horace B. Packer in 1942, the house was cut in two, the land divided and each piece sold separately.

14 Continue along Main Street to Charles Street, then turn right one block to Pearl Street. On the opposite corner is **St. Paul's Episcopal Church**. The parish was organized in 1838 and the present

15 The building at 55 Pearl Street was erected about 1846 as the office of the **Bingham Estate**, a land company. It was moved from its original site in 1897 when **St. Paul's Episcopal Church** was built.

16 Across Central Avenue is a block of red brick buildings, in which la firms and insurance companies have their offices. These buildings date back to the 1860's and 1870's and several were built with law offices the street floor and living quarters upstairs. This was the case with 19 Cent Avenue, which was built by the Honorable Mortimer F. Elliot, who served a congressman-at-large in the Forty-eighth Congress, now the law offices of **Cox, Stokes and Lantz, P.C.**

17 Walk three blocks down Main Street to our **central business district**. Almost all of these buildings date back to the last century. Main houses are second and third generation family-owned businesses. **Dunham's Department Store** and **Café 1905**, built in 1905 by Roy & Fannie Dunham, is still owned and operated by the Dunham family.

18 Across East Avenue is the **Wellsboro Diner**, which opened in 193 This is a fine example of the diners of the 1930's and is more uniqu in that it has been in continuous operation as a diner and has never been removed from its original site.

19 Located next to the **Diner** is the former **Shattuck House**. Completed in 1909, this house is one of the last three homes in wh was one of Wellsboro's beautiful tree-lined residential sections on lower Main Street. The building is now home to an Antique shop.

20 The **Sherwood Motel**, formerly the house of Walter Sherwood, E and family, the son of the Hon. Henry Sherwood and US Congressn The **Sherwood House** was built circa 1886. It was converted to a motel 1952. The house is the oldest of the three remaining houses on lower Mai Street and is the only one that is still a residence.

21 Crossing the street again to the corner of Main and Queen Streets, you will find the **United Methodist Church**. This building was completed in 1905.

22 The Art Deco **Arcadia Theatre**, at 50 Main Street, was built in 19

A Bunch of Good Stuff
March 17

I have been without my computer now for two whole days and it's like my best friend, whom I do have issues with now and then, has abandoned me. Shane came and picked it up Saturday morning and you have no idea how many times I have walked over to my desk to enter something for my book only to see the empty space where it used to be smiling at me.

Go back to Saturday:

I had to find a way to fill my day so I remembered that Mahjong was played at the Pop Culture Shop at 2 East Avenue on Tuesdays and Saturdays. That little store really seems to do a big business. They carry games of every sort for people of all ages and eras. The owners are very nice and friendly people…they fit right in with the

Wellsboro that I have come to love…but something unforeseen happened while I was there this time.

Inside that shop there are two sections of it, one in front and then another where we play Mahjong. In there, there is an eight-foot wall between that room and the bookstore next door. Above that wall the ceiling is about twelve feet high so there is space between the two shops from the top of the wall to the ceiling.

The wall

I had ordered a book from the bookstore a few days before this and was waiting for a call from Kasey to let me know when it was in. Well, while playing Mahjong my phone rang and it was Kasey, but by the time I answered it she was leaving a message for me and I could hear her doing it. I yelled at her over the top of that wall that I'd be in after my game to pick it up and she yelled back at me, "OK."

I thought nothing of it and after I finished playing and as I was leaving the game store the owner, Julian, asked me to wait a minute. I stopped and he told me that Kasey and Kevin (book store owners) and them are having a feud…and it seems that it is a very bad feud, just short of being a Hatfield and McCoy feud (no shotguns as yet).

I told him that he was popping my bubble because I thought that I had found my Shangri-La, my dream town. He assured me that it certainly was and that they were going to do everything that they could to keep it that way. That was so disappointing. That was the second disappointment that I had since December 28th–the date when I first moved here. Let's see, in two-and-one-half months and two disappointments. I guess that's not too bad.

Now up to Sunday:

Today, I decided that I would go to the Episcopal Church, it being the church that my ancestors attended. I also wanted to ask the priest if he could possibly get that same archive that he showed me when I first got here. I wanted to see if there were any Jones' in there. I looked at the pictures of them that I have already and found that in December of 1860 John Sofield (my great-great-grandpa) got baptized and as I found out not long ago, they were living in the next county over and his mother-in-law lived with them and her name was Betsy Weeks.

In the baptismal book it has the name of a Mrs. Weeks about three names down under his on the same date. I'll just bet that was her. (Evidence? Hmmm, maybe.) I supposed that when you are doing your genealogy you want things to go a certain way and when you find something like that, it probably wouldn't stand up in court but you still grab on to it (circumstantial evidence) and hate to let go. I will go over there to the church Thursday when they are having their weekly rummage sale and see if he found those books.

The Presbyterian Church

I arrived a little late for the service and it is so like the Catholic Church. In fact, in one of their books that you are supposed to recite, you are supposed to say that you believe in the Catholic Church. For simplicity sake, I will refer to the priest as Father Hinton as that is the title that he takes.

There was a short sermon and a lot of good music and then it was over and the people started going to the cafeteria for refreshments and that is when I took the pictures of the stained glass windows and got a very good shot of the altar.

The altar

While I was sitting in there looking around I started fantasizing about how over 160 years ago my relatives were here...not in this physical building, but here religiously and only across the street where the Episcopalian Church was back then and I felt so fortunate for just being here...here in Wellsboro and here in their church, that the tears started coming out and I couldn't stop them. I wasn't boo-hooing but just tearing up. I really got emotional.

Then I went to the cafeteria and had a little food and sat with some ladies that told me things that I had wanted to know. One of them was where the fire station was in the early to mid-1800s and they knew right away. This is where my great-granduncle, James Sofield, had worked as a fireman when he was killed in that train wreck. Here is a picture of it below. Behind it you can see the present fire station.

The old fire station

After a few minutes Father Hinton came in dressed in a beautiful purple robe. When you talk to him, he is so different from the way he is on the platform. He is so down to Earth. I had asked him if Episcopalian Priests were allowed to be married and he said, "Oh yes, and sorry I am already taken." Then he laughed so hard he was bending over. It was so funny. Here he is in all his glory and still laughing:

Father Hinton

It seems that everywhere I go to meet new people I learn something else to share in my book. I learn as much if not more from the local people here than I do in my computer searches.

The book that I purchased from the bookstore was a "picture only" book and it was called Life in Wellsboro, 1880-1920. I couldn't wait to get home to read it, or I should say, "Look at the pictures." There is a page that shows how the firemen in that day (1800s, before cars) had to do a lot of running. They would have practice runs. The below photograph was taken around 1893 which is about fifteen years after James Sofield was a fireman there. I can imagine that in those days they even had it harder.

And now, Monday:

Today I spent a lot of time doing some computer work for Brian. Then I went to the surveyor's company to pick up the items that I asked them to do for me and that was identifying the house, for sure, on the corner of King and Main as being the one that Ezekiel Jones owned and sold to Joseph Sofield. This still leaves me perplexed as to where Joseph Sofield and family and Helen Jones (Sofield) were living when she was nineteen in 1850. I think that the only way that I am going to find out for sure is if they will just come back for a little while and tell me.

(Hey, if anyone out there is listening, I was only foolin', I don't want any bumps in the night…ok?)

Aerial photograph of King Street and Main Street

From there I rode to the HOUSE WITH THE RED DOOR. I got out and took some pictures of it. This is the red door that an old letter of a relative of the Shearers who bought the home in the 1800s were written about that Mary Todd Lincoln gave them as a gift when they moved here to Wellsboro from Springfield, Illinois. That letter is the only "proof" that I know of that makes this story true. As I said before, even with circumstantial evidence we like to hang on to it, and hang on to it I will. After all, my circumstantial great-great-grandfather Ezekiel Jones was the first white man to own the property. Doesn't that make me something?

The house with the red door

The Meeting!
March 20

This whole month is Lent. I am not sure how the religions all practice it but the way they do it here is very unusual. They hold the services every Wednesday at the Presbyterian Church but every week there is a speaker from all different denominations. Two weeks ago it was a 7th Day Adventist minister, then last week it was from the Lutheran Church and yesterday it was a Catholic Priest from St. Peters Catholic Church.

After a half hour sermon those in the congregation went to the cafeteria where they served some food. This time, though, the organizers for the upcoming Bucktail Reunion fest were there. Matt Herring and his grandfather were there. As I have mentioned before, Matt Herring is the chief organizer for the upcoming reunion. His grandfather is also a re-enactor who is also a preacher in real life along with playing the part of the Reverend Calkins, the actual chaplain in the 149th Company A.

Matt Herring and Yours Truly

I also learned that, that same original chaplain had been the preacher in this very church here in Wellsboro before he enlisted in the war in 1862. It was over two years ago when Leslie, Brian and I were touring Gettysburg that we met that tour guide, also Reverend Calkins, who was the great-great-grandson of the original. This Gettysburg/Wellsboro family is getting tighter and tighter all the time. It's like history and today is blending in together through lineage.

Before we went down to eat, the photographer from the local press approached us. They led us out in front of the church and took our pictures and they will be coming out in the Wellsboro Gazette soon. I was there to represent Captain Alfred Sofield and it was a very proud moment for me.

After that we went inside and I was introduced to a lady from the press that took my name address and phone number so she could contact me later for an interview. It was all quite exciting. These re-enactors are so dedicated to this cause that they treat me and other ancestors with so much respect and honor that it makes you feel like you are the one that actually were there and did the fighting, all the while in your mind you are thinking that it was just an accident of birth, but swaddling in it anyway.

Left to Right: Matt Herring, 7th Day Adventist Priest, Catholic Priest

Matt was telling the others and me in the meeting that the day before he found out how to contact me last month he had been in Gettysburg and had just put a coin on my great-grandfather's grave. I guess that is something that they do in honor of that particular soldier. I am usually not the type of person that is much into symbols, but I must admit, that in this case and in the case of all my ancestors here in Wellsboro, I have found myself enveloped in it and loving it.

After I got home, still glowing from the afternoon, Robert Wagner came by to pick me up for the Civil War Round Table meeting in Mansfield. He brought along two other riders and one was a former doctor/surgeon that lives right up the street from me. He looked to be about my age and also a very nice looking man. He is also a Civil War enthusiast and is writing a book for his posterity only—it's about WWII. As we kept talking he talked about how he was going to be going to Maryland to visit a grandchild and then a couple of weeks later he and his wife were going to go to France.

I asked him if it didn't bother him to travel and at that point, Roger asked me to guess the man's age and I guessed it to be about my age. Come to find out he is 94. Wow, then he started telling us how he takes long walks daily and gets up early and first thing he does is to go swimming. In my head I started giving myself excuses for not doing those things, but they are all true. I am allergic to the chlorine in swimming pools (I don't want to hear about your Aunt Mary who has a salt water pool, ok?), and when I take walks my hips start hurting before I even make it to the corner. That is the truth, but I just wonder if I'd do it if they didn't hurt. Guess I'll never know.

When we arrived at the round table and went in, there was, as always, all sorts of sweet goodies sitting on the counter. How can I stay healthy and eat all those goodies? It's like I have no choice in the matter. If they're there, I must eat them. Just think, there are people starving in Africa! I did notice, though, that the men that I came with didn't eat any. I only had two cookies and some coffee, BUT NO SUGAR! Now I'm sure to lose weight.

At the meeting I was allowed to stand up and tell the group why I was in Wellsboro and that I was writing my book. I also told them about what I learned about the upcoming reunion in August and that they were looking for ancestors of the local Civil War soldiers. There was a man there that, after I sat down, pointed to me and told me that the 149th Bucktails were no more than copycats of the original ones and that back then there was a lot of controversy about that. It kind of hurt my feelings but another man stood up and said, "No matter, they paid with their blood." It became very still after that. I thought that the first comment was, under the circumstances, out of place.

No, Wellsboro didn't lose any points because I was in Mansfield. After that they showed the second half of a Lincoln movie that was very good. I had already read the book The Lincoln Years that covered the years from his presidency to his death. It's a book by Carl Sandburg. It was very good movie *and* book.

Today I walked over to the Episcopal Church to see if the baptismal archive book was available to see but Father Hinton had forgotten to get it for me but the secretary told me that she would have it up there tomorrow for me.

I went downstairs to their weekly rummage sale and it was quite nice. I bought a few little things and I had a nice time talking genealogy to the ladies who work there. I really enjoyed the visit. Then I walked home and believe it or not it had been snowing again. This is the 20th of March…and it's snowing.

When I got home there were two guests staying here in one of the upstairs guest rooms. I met them later in the day. Nice people from York, PA where Brian and I had worked a couple of years ago. I asked them what brought them to Wellsboro and they said that after 9/11 they took a trip and ended up here and fell in love with it from that day on. The lady, Eileen, said that when they ended up here in Wellsboro, that there was something about it that gave them peace. She said, as she inhaled deeply and let it out as if relaxing, that she felt as if, "this is home." I know that feeling and I love it when others say the same thing. I told you that it was a Never Never Land.

The Letter (And More)
March 26

I finally got up the courage to write the letter to the owners who live in the house with the red door. I have had the information from the surveyor's office back for a week and I just couldn't seem to figure out how and what I was going to say to them...I even had to figure out what I wanted. I knew that I wanted a connection between my history and that house. Here is what I finally wrote:

March 23, 2014
Dear Owners,

Allow me to introduce myself to you. My name is Audrey Sofield Barber. I know that there has been a lot of talk about your house, the main reason being that the Red Door was given to the owners of the property, i.e.: The Shearers from Springfield, IL. by Mary Todd Lincoln, back in the 1800s.

To get to my point, let me begin by telling you what brought me to Wellsboro. It was about 11 years ago I began doing my genealogy while living in Utah and in doing so I received a phone call from a man in Omaha, NE, that told me that he was a cousin of mine and that our ancestors came from Wellsboro, PA. He also told me that my great-grandfather, Alfred Sofield, had been the Justice of the Peace here in the 1850s and 60's. In 1862 he became the first recruiter here in Tioga County for the Civil War and became the captain of the 149th Company A of the Bucktails. That was in August of 1862 and in July on 1863 he was killed in Gettysburg and is buried there.

Since that time, my husband and I had been living on Maui and one day he got a call from Williams Pipeline Company in Bethlehem, PA, to come for a job in the real estate department, as he had done that before. Subsequently, we moved to Stroudsburg and lived there for a year and then he was moved to work in New Jersey. During the holidays we took a trip up here to Wellsboro and fell in love with this place. I had been working on my genealogy all this time but I wanted to be closer to the actual place where they lived and closer to the Historical Society and the Courthouse so that I could pull up deeds, et cetera, to see where they lived. It was decided that I would move here and write a book about what I was doing and what I have found out and <u>am</u> finding out almost every day that I am here.

One thing that I found out while pulling deeds is that one of the first few people who started here in Wellsboro in the very early 1800s was an Ezekiel Jones. Jones began by purchasing many properties along Main Street and then up to King Street and to Walnut Street. I also found in my searches that my great-grandmother, the wife of Alfred Sofield was previously Helen Jones. The first property that Mr. Jones purchased was the very property that you are living on. It was the corner of Main and King. I actually hired a surveyor, Cunningham Land Services, to assure me that my assumption was a correct one...and it was. I still wasn't absolutely sure if there was a connection between Ezekiel Jones and my great-grandmother until it got a little clearer in an 1844 deed that showed that Mr. Jones sold that same property (yours) to Joseph Sofield who was related to my great-grandfather and that in 1850, my great-grandmother was living in the same household as Joseph Sofield and his wife, Pheobe Sofield, nee Jones. I feel strongly that my relatives lived in that house, your house, as it was in those days although, I know for a fact, that it has been very much refurbished and made into the beautiful house that it is today. Ezekiel Jones not only lived there but had his blacksmith business there too and at the time, the property went clear back to Water Street. I sit here sometimes in the sunroom where my computer is and stare out the window at that house and my imagination goes wild. I imagine my great-grandmother as a nineteen-year-old teenager going in and out of there.

This is the 1850 census:

Name:	Joseph Sofield	
Age:	32	
Birth Year:	abt 1818	
Birthplace:	New York	
Home in 1850:	Wellsboro, Tioga, Pennsylvania	
Gender:	Male	
Family Number:	80	
	Name	**Age**
	Joseph Sofield	32
	Phebee Sofield	38
	Wallace Sofield	8
Household Members:	Charles Sofield	6
	Alice Sofield	4
	Helen M Jones	19
	Thaddeus Finch	17
	Eunice Mudge	16
	Benj Sofield	63

There is only one catch in these findings: in the deed showing the purchase from Jones to Sofield on Oct. 2, 1844, the next deed over it shows that Sofield sold it to a man named Joseph Sanders on the same day and for the same price. Now he may have rented back or...I can't think of any other reason that was done but I still can't get it out of my mind that they may have lived there. I am putting this information into my book and with your permission I'd like to have my picture taken with you that I can also enter in there.

I would love to meet you both in person as I am living across the street in the old Packer House Inn, a B&B, 133 Main Street. It is owned by Nelle Rounseville as she rented the whole house to me until May 28th, when all the tourists start coming in. I know that I will be here in Wellsboro at least until after August as that is when they are having the Bucktail Reunion here and I will be taking orders for my completed book in the Green at that time and will also take part in the program as an ancestor of a Bucktail.

If it is agreeable to meet with you, my phone number is 808.346.7549.

Sincerely, Audrey Sofield Barber

P.S. If we meet, I will show you the deeds and the work that Cunningham did on it.

So now: the waiting game. Am I going to get a response? If so, will it be a "Welcome to Wellsboro" response? Or will it be a "Don't bother me" response? I am ready for that to happen. (Editor's note: as of the time of this printing, there has been no response.)

Now on another tack, today it is March 26th and I woke up to about two or three inches of snow and it is snowing now as we speak, or I should say, "as I write." This is the strangest weather that I have ever been in, but, of course, I have only lived in "snow country" other than Pennsylvania, once and that was Utah but at least when I lived in Utah they had Spring when Spring was supposed to be Spring. This is winter when it's supposed to be spring. Whether people believe in climate change or not...the climate, she's a chang'n. As uncomfortably as going out in the cold can be, it is still beautiful as I look out the windows.

Here is the forecast for the week:

This is sweet little Amanda out shoveling snow on March 26, 2014.

How I love the picture on the previous page. This is a typical Pennsylvania Mennonite scene that reeks of coziness. Every morning when I get up (and it's early) I hear the back door open at around 6:30 or 7:00 and here comes Amanda in the section of the kitchen where she does her secretarial duties that last only about fifteen minutes.

I saunter (rush) in there to talk to her, knowing that I can't talk to her for very long as she has other duties to do, as you can see from the picture. She not only does the bookwork for this B&B that I am in but also for the one on the corner that Nelle also owns. Then there is another one next door to me that also serves as a B&B under Nelle's guidance along with some cabins a ways out of town that Amanda takes care of. She has been working in this capacity since she was fifteen years old and she is now twenty-five.

Amanda hasn't had much schooling as she is from a pretty large family and is the only girl. She is a hard worker and is the sweetest, most naïve person that I have ever met. When I talk to her in the mornings I usually tell her about bits and pieces of the happenings in the world. In her mind she lives in a cocoon of sorts. Her little experience with the comings and goings of the world, or even the community are like looking through rose-colored glasses.

I try to be careful not to tell her too many negative things but I have told her of the Civil War and about slavery as it was then and how Lincoln freed them. I told her about how Wellsboro played an important part in the horrible war. She had no idea, and she lives right here where there are statues and memorials in The Green that is a block away from here.

I think that I would like to live in Amanda's world, to a degree…as it's a happy world. I do think, although, that some knowledge of the history of her little town would be a benefit. When I talk to her about things, she just drinks it in. She loves to have knowledge but is so enveloped in her duties that she loves that I don't think that she feels that she is missing anything. Actually I feel that I am missing something that she has: complete contentedness (at least that is what I see). She gets excited over the littlest things. Last night as I was watching TV my cell phone made a texting sound and when I opened it, it was a little song that Amanda had sent me. She warms my heart.

Every Wednesday during Lent, as I had mentioned before, they have a short, half hour sermon given by a minister of another church. It starts at noon and today the Methodist Minister gave the sermon called "Patience and Self Control." He began by telling a little joke, although it didn't have anything to do with patience nor self-control. He said that a man came over here from a third world country and went shopping for the first time. He noticed how many prepared foods there were. First he picked up powdered milk and read the instructions where it said, "mix with water and you have milk." Wow, they don't even need a cow," he thinks. Then he finds powdered orange juice and read the label where it said, "just mix with water and you have orange juice." He thought: "Wow, you have orange juice and you don't even need an orange tree!" Then he went around to another aisle and picked up baby powder…use your imagination. Anyway it started the sermon out with a little levity.

Afterwards we went downstairs and they had two soups for us to choose from, one was a nice chicken and rice soup and the other one was a thick, milk-based creamy type soup. It looked good, but remember, I went to Weight Watchers last night and I didn't want to blow it. I sat at a table where some of the Methodist Church members sat and the lady across from me was very nice and friendly. She was telling me how their church (Methodist) was dividing up into groups to do various community things and hers was called Outreach. She was telling me that there is a homeless shelter here in Wellsboro and told me where it is. She said that because the funds are so limited that they have a bus that comes every late afternoon and picks up the approximately twelve homeless people. The bus takes them to the shelter; they eat, talk and then go to bed. The next morning they are picked up again and taken back to town to roam the streets until they are picked up in the evening. There isn't enough money to keep the place open all day by paying the extra utilities and paying someone there to watch over them, feed them in the morning and afternoon, too. It wouldn't be quite so bad but it is freezing here, even in the daytime. This lady that I met is Pat Wells Newruck, and she, herself goes down there to deliver their evening meal and talk to them.

Pat Wells Newruck

Pat thinks that she may be a descendent of Mary Wells, who Wellsboro is named after. I may help her find out. She's a very sweet lady. The man in the background to the left with the long hair and the beard is the minister of the Presbyterian Church. He is a very charismatic man, very likable. Everyone that I've met here is likable. Hang on to that other shoe, Audrey, as you don't want it to drop!

I Don't Even Have To Leave Home!
April 4

I have let a few days go by without reporting to my readers because I hadn't gone anywhere to gather more material. What I didn't realize is, I didn't really have to go anywhere. Sometimes all I have to do is just read the paper. If you will remember back in the first part of this book I talked about how I went to St. Paul's Episcopal Church because I had found that there were a lot of my Sofield clan in there. The last time I went I saw that the first pages in the archive book were for families and that Alfred Sofield and family was in there; however, that was the last I saw his name but saw the rest of the family all through there. The archive book starts with families then goes to Baptisms, Confirmations, marriages and on to funerals.

I had noticed that the same Reverend Marple had done it all. He started with baptisms and there were plenty of children baptized. Then ending it with funerals, I remember thinking to myself, "he must have been very old by the time they had reached funeral ages. He buried my great-great-grandparents.

Now to the point….while reading the Wellsboro Gazette this morning I came across some announcements for workshop activities for the week. The From My Shelf's bookstore always has interesting things going on that they announce in the paper. This advertisement talks about what's coming up, titled, "Dates Given for Writers group, and Author Event."

The writers group is an extension of the one that I attended last month and I loved it. But the second part interested me greatly, i.e.: "Author Event." It seems that there is an author that is going to be there named Gloria Marple! I immediately got on the phone and called Kasey at the bookstore and she told me that the Marple families have been here in Wellsboro for generations. I can't wait to meet with her, plus she's an author and maybe can give me some advice. I have a less than sneaky suspicion that she is a relative of Reverend Maple that baptized, confirmed, married and buried my relatives.

I will be going to a musical play at the Warehouse, across the street again. I called Lin, one of my Mahjong playing partners and she is going to meet me there. Can't wait to get back with pictures and tell you about it. I am trying to catch up on some much needed culture. My mother's life was full of culture, especially anything to do with music. As I was growing up she was always taking me to musical concerts or contests. She even took me to Hollywood to an opera one time. She gave me some opera glasses to look around and see if I saw anyone that looked famous. Lo and behold I saw Jane Withers (thank you Google as I went there and entered Josephine the Plumber and up came Jane Withers). We rushed down to the lobby at intermission to get her autograph but the crowd around her was too large and my mom didn't want to miss the second half of the opera. To tell you the truth, to me opera is very much like rap insofar as you can't understand what is being said or sung about.

What I do every week is to go to town and pick up brochures of happenings here in Wellsboro and also go to the newspaper and get my calendar out jot down the events that I want to attend. It's fun doing that. Yesterday I walked to town and thought that I would start looking for some suitable clothes to buy for the August Bucktail Reunion. The first place that I went to was The Fifth Season, rightfully named because it is connected to the Deane Center, which is the cultural center for this whole area. That whole building used to house the Agitator and is where my granduncle worked as a teenager.

The inside of the building is very modern with state of the art sound systems, stages dance floors and a huge entry lobby with comfortable armchairs scattered about. Then there is a door that goes directly into the clothing store. The fifth season carries very nice clothes and the atmosphere is charming. I purchased two pairs of beautiful long flowing pants, a blouse and a darling coat.

While I was paying for the items, the pretty, young girl that waited on me and I started talking. It ended up where I told her why I was here and what I was doing. I mentioned the letter that I had written to the owners of the house with the red door and how they hadn't answered and lo and behold, she and her husband are friends of theirs. They both belong to the Rotary Club. She said that they travel a lot and they will surely be back next week as they are having dinner with them. She will mention me to them. I'm very anxious to see the outcome of that event.

Here is Rachel Tews at her beautiful store on Main Street

From there I went to my friend Toni's Natural Ways store. She carries natural and organic items and now a clothing retail store has brought in some clothes to that store, too. I like it over there. It's cozy. On one side you take care of your health and on the other side you dress up nicely. The clothing section is called Shabby Rue 2, or Rue 2. It has some cute things in there. A wine company is supposed to be coming in with their locally grown wine real soon

Shabby Rue has a main store on Main Street and the lady who owns it is very friendly. I went in there, too, one day and met and talked with her for a long time. In fact I went in there yesterday on the way to Natural Ways and found something that I wanted to try on but there is only one dressing room and it was taken. As I turned to leave I found it to be the organ player at the Presbyterian Church. (Her piano playing is absolutely enviable.) She's very friendly and then we started talking. Now here's the odd part—to me anyway: she is a member of the Methodist Church and plays the piano at the Presbyterian Church on Sundays. I have never seen such interdenominational fervor in my life. I have only been here in Wellsboro for two months and I am already running into friends at the store and other places. I just love this familial feeling that most people have here.

April 5

I found this article today in an old newspaper. It's about a fire that happened here in 1874. What it did was to give me a clue as to where my great-grandmother had a shop.

The citizens had only partially recovered from the shock, when on the morning of April 1st 1874, another fire occurred, which was still more destructive than the first, sweeping away the entire square of buildings between Crafton and Walnut streets back to Pearl street. The fire was first discovered in the store of William Wilson, and it was not ascertained positively how it originated. It was said at the time that many heard the alarm; but, it being on the 1st of April it was thought to be a device to "fool" them, and the fire became unmanageable before the true state of affairs was understood. The principal losers were Cobb & Bache, H. W. Williams, A. Foley, Dr. L. M. Johnson, L. A. Gardner, W. T. Mathews, Charles Toles, M. Watkins, Nichols & Seeley, William Wilson, L. B. Reynolds, the Nichols estate, C. J. Wheeler, C. C. Mathers, Mrs. A. J. Sofield, Guttenberg & Co., N. P.

Close, J. R. Anderson, Mathers & Bodine C. G. Osgood, Robinson & Co., W. B. Van Horn, Harkness & Burnett, E. H. Wood, A. L. Bodine, J. Johnson, Mrs. Hatkins, Mrs. Carey J. Etner, William Hill, Bowen & Fisher, S. B. Warriner, E. H. Hastings, William Riley, Mrs. Mary Lamb, M. M. Converse, Wheeler & Wilcox, David Carr, ------ Bunnell, G. W. Navle, John Grey, Seth Watkins, C. L. Wilcox, William Roberts and W. E. Pierson.

It's so amazing though, because when I go to see Toni at her little shop, she is on Crafton Street. Walnut Street is two blocks behind Pearl Street and is one block behind me. This article gives me another clue where my great-grandmother probably had her millinery store in 1874, nine years after her husband was killed.

Notice some of the last names of people that were affected by the fire. There was "Bache." I have a picture in here of his great-granddaughter. Then there is "Seeley." I have talked to the Seeleys on the phone. Next is "Sofield" and you know who that is. Then there is "Bodine." I have talked to him, he is the Chief of Police here and that is his great-great-grand relative in the article. Last but not least there was S. B. Warriner. Captain Warriner was the captain right under my great-grandfather in the 149th and I have spoken to his relative on the phone.

Salute d'Amour
April 9

Of all days that I couldn't quickly grab my iPad, it was today. I called Celia and told her that I had borrowed a book from her friend and that I would like to get it back to her ASAP. She told me that the Gmeiner Art & Cultural Center at 134 Main Street (as you can see by the address, is right across the street again from me), was going to have a concert at 10AM. I rushed around to get ready, as I love concerts, and couldn't find my iPad that I had just used five minutes previously.

I quickly got dressed and rushed over there just as they were starting. There was a beautiful Chinese young lady on piano (Wow! What a player!) and another young man on the violin and another on the cello. Then came time for a tall, handsome Chinese man for a violin solo. He played Salute d'Amour and my tears started flowing and I only had a little piece of tissue to wipe my wet mascara off with.

Songs that are played in minor keys bring on the tears. It was beautiful. Oh, how I wish that I had had my iPad for pictures but woe and alas I didn't. When I was growing up, my parents and paternal grandmother were musicians. My dad, another Alfred Sofield, played violin and had never had a lesson. He even read music. He liked to play classical tunes and when this man, today, played that song it just brought back so many memories...thus, the tears.

Just as I came home I had a message from Anja who owns the Pop Culture Store where we play Mahjongg. She wanted me to come over there today and play. She also wants me to join then on Friday and Saturday for more MahJong. Whew, that game can be very habit forming and so I went. We had a good time and that is what I look forward to. I have gotten so many good friends since I've been here that it's almost like I've lived here all my life.

Tonight I will be going to the Writers Meeting at the bookstore. I loved that meeting so much last time that I am anxious to attend. Tonight we are supposed to read the first five pages of any book that we are or have written and then it will be critiqued. (I'm also going to try to slip in the introduction if they let me). That critiquing part I can do without but I guess it's better now than when it's finished and people read part of it and throw the rest away.

I find that I write just like I talk. It's like having a conversation with people, even though it is one sided. My husband tells me that a lot of my conversations are one sided...my side. I hope that is not true because I am interested in people and hearing their stories. Anyway, what you see is what you get in this book.

Kasey Cox Cooledge, owner of "From My Shelf Books & Gifts"

Last night at the writers meeting I walked the almost five blocks there (I'm a whimp). I love that meeting and there are so many interesting people that attend. There were eleven of us there last night. I was anxious and yet apprehensive about reading my introduction and first three pages of the book...but I was chosen by Kasey to be the first one to read. After I finished reading the introduction, I ask if I should go on because we had a shortage of time. The woman next to me said, "By all means go on, I can't wait to hear the rest of it." Well, that sat very well with me so I continued.

After it was over Kasey asked if anyone had any thoughts on it and they all seemed to like it. Kasey really gave me some rave reviews. She went on to tell them all how a couple years ago I had come in there with my husband and told her of my love of Wellsboro and my ancestral history here and that I had wanted so badly to write about it. She said that it took me a long time to get to this point but that she loved it. She said that because of the quaintness of this town, she regularly has people come in there wanting and actually writing about it, and then she said, "But having said that, Audrey's flows in a conversational manner that tops all the others that I have read." I couldn't believe it. My heart was actually pounding with excitement. When it was time to walk home I had to call Brian and tell him about it. I was walking about two inches off the sidewalk. It was a beautiful evening, about 9:30 PM, and the moon was a little over half full. There was a just right breeze to compliment the situation and that was my night last night.

A Little Side Story
April 12

It seems that my feet and lower legs are always cold and while I am playing Mahjongg I'll lean down and try to warm them. One day one of the nice ladies that I play with named June asked me what the problem was and I told her of my plight. She said that she used to have the same problem but that she got leggings or leg warmers. I asked where you can get them and she said that you'd probably have to send for them, but she had so many that she would bring me a pair. (This is how one copes in a town without a mall, people actually help one another)

A couple of days later she did just that. I started wearing them right away and what a difference! This morning I knew that I had to go wash my hair and take a shower so that I could be ready for today's Mahjongg game at noon. I hopped in the shower and washed my hair and with this shampoo that I am using, you are supposed to leave it in while you continue your shower…so I did. As I looked down to wash my legs, what do you think that I saw? Yes, you probably already guessed it…there they were dripping wet: my leggings! That is how comfortable they are. I know that this has nothing to do with the Civil War, nor Wellsboro but it may help you understand why my kids call me Lucy. That's for another book.

Spring and a Play
April 13

I looked at the calendar and couldn't find which day in April when the first day of spring would be...but I can tell you when it was for Wellsboro! It was April 13th! I thought that it would never arrive but it came.

I actually got out and walked the whole seven blocks to the pharmacy to pick up a prescription and back. For me, that is aerobic! While walking I can't ever seem to make it to my destination without spending money though. The only way I could do that is not to bring my money with me, but how was I going to pay for my prescription? So I brought $80. (My prescription was $6, but you never know how much it's going to be until you get there...right?) I stopped in Dunham's Department Store and had fun looking around. I bought a few things but the really interesting part was looking at the people out in their shorts and flip flops...some pushing strollers, some riding motorcycles that have probably been sitting in their garages all winter. This is the first time that I have either visited or lived in Wellsboro that it wasn't in a cold season. I'm sure I will love them all except in the heat of summer. I am not a summer person...don't like heat. Today, though, it was probably in the mid-70s...just right!

I strolled around town, looking at all the buildings and as usual trying to figure out which ones were probably seen by my ancestors. I have recently purchased a book called *Life in Wellsboro 1880-1920* and it is basically a picture book of Wellsboro with pictures that were taken between those two eras. When looking at the pictures, you can see that the buildings' windows are the same, as are the top architectural designs. They are probably the same actual buildings.

What I've done is to write down the pages in the book that were taken of the downtown and go to them and see what they are now. The main differences are the modernization of the sidewalks, the pretty center divider with its gaslights down Main Street; of course, the shops have upgraded their storefronts to a degree and there are no more muddy streets. Horse manure in the roads has been replaced by clean paved streets. It would have been nice if the old photographs could have been in color so that we could see more of the beauty of that day like you see in period movies.

There is another interesting portion of that book and it is called "The Wellsboro Directory 1890-1920." It's like a telephone book without telephones. The page that I have scanned for you is describing what the symbols denote.

Wellsboro Borough Directory, 1899

EXPLANATIONS

Directory is arranged as follows: 1st, name of individual or firm; 2d, post office address in parenthesis, if different from the name of the town; 3d, the figures following the letter r indicate the number of the road on which the party resides and will be found by reference to the map in the back part of this work; where no road number is given, the party is supposed to reside in the village; 4th, business or occupation; 5th, figures placed after the occupation of a farmer indicate the number of acres owned or leased; 6th, names in **bold type** are those who have kindly given their patronage to the work and without whose aid its publication would have been impossible.

ABBREVIATIONS — Adv., advertisement; asst., assistant; ave., avenue; bds., boards; bldg., building; cor., corner; Co., company; do., ditto; E., east; h., house; ins., insurance; manuf., manufacturer; mfg., manufacturing; n., near; N., north; pres., president; R. R., railroad; Ry., railway; S., south; W., west; com. trav., commercial traveler; emp., employee.

Adams Nettie (Mrs Walter C) cigarmaker, h 75 Main
Adams Walter C, brakeman F B Ry, bds Coles House
Aker Francis E, glass blower, h 39 East ave
Albert Henry V, meat cutter Fischler Bros, h over 96 Main
Alexander C Austin, engineer F B Ry, h Jackson
Alexander Harriet A, dressmaker Jackson, h do
Alexander Sophia C, widow John, h Jackson
Allen Edward, carpenter, h Pearl
Allen Elizabeth C, widow Thomas, h 24 East ave
Allen William D, (Spencer & Allen) h Crafton
Allington Isaac, teamster, h Nichols cor Sears
American Express Co, A A Truman agt, 65 Main
Andrews Alfred A, glass blower, h Austin
Andrews Francis S, carpenter and farmer 14, h Kelsey
Andrews Laura M, school teacher, bds Cone
Andrews William R, glass blower, h Cone
Arey Sarah, widow Wiliam R, h East ave
Atherton Gilbert C, teamster, h Austin
Atherton Marvin W, laborer, h Austin
Austin Benjamin F, farmer, leases of Robert R Austin 110, h Central ave n boro line
AUSTIN M G & CO (Milo G A and Mrs Charlotte S. Coles) groceries, fruits, provisions, crockery, lamps, glassware, &c 90 Main
AUSTIN MILO G (M G A & Co) h 47 Central ave
AUSTIN ROBERT G manager M G Austin & Co, 90 Main, h 53 Central ave
Austin Robert H, school teacher, bds 25 Grant
Austin Robert R, farmer 110, h 25 Grant
74

Avery Cyrus W, farmer 80, h Kelsey
Avery Jeannette Mrs, h Queen
Avery William O, teamster, h 37 Water
Babcock Charles L, registrar and recorder county office bldg, Main, h Walnut
Bache John N, real estate, h 4 Charles
Bache William, h 55 Pearl
BACHE WILLIAM JR (Nichols & Bache) h 37 Main
Bacon Leon, emp cider mill, bds 23 Conway
BACON MORGAN L SR, physician and surgeon, health officer, graduate Long Island College, Main n Queen, h do
BACON M LOUIS JR, physician and surgeon, eye specialist, graduate University of Buffalo, Main n Queen, h do
Bacon Oliver, farmer in Delmar 390, h Morris cor Bacon
BACON SETH, propr Wellsboro cider and vinegar works, Purple cor Cone, h 23 Conway
Bailey Arthur L, law student, bds. 69 Pearl
Bailey Frank W, clerk 37 Main, bds Austin
Bailey Harry F, school teacher, bds 69 Pearl
BAILEY & HOWE (Ransom W B & Morris D H) dealers in wagons, harness, agricultural implements, fertilizers, etc, 12-16 Waln
Bailey Llellyn L, life and accident insurance and real estate and farmer 120, Central ave, h 69 Pearl
BAILEY MYRON F, furniture and undertaking, wagons, harness and farm implements, first class livery, owner of stock farm, 75, in Charleston, breeder and dealer in thoroughbred Jersey cattle and dealer in horses, sheep, etc, 37 Main, h Austin
BAILEY RANSOM W (B & Howe), 10 cows, farmer, 125, in Charleston, h Charleston cor McInroy
Bailey Wallace J, agt Osborn Machine Co, stock dealer, h East ave n limits
Baker Carrie L Mrs, domestic, 32 West ave
Baker Edward, farmer, h Bodine
Baker Frank, farmer, 53, h Bodine
Baker Frank L, glass packer, farmer, 24, h Bodine
Baker Joseph C, farmer on shares for L L Bailey, 123, h Bagley Lane
Baker Thomas S, painter and paper hanger, h Bodine
Baker William S, painter, bds Bodine
BARNES AUGUSTUS F (B & Roy) h Charleston
BARNES & ROY (Augustus F B & Arthur M R) publishers and props The Wellsboro Agitator and job printers, 104 Main
Barnum Grace B, dressmaker, bds Fellows ave
Barnum Julia, widow Abram, h Fellows ave
Bastian Katharine, widow Samuel, dressmaker, h Water
Battner Matthew, h Tioga
Beach James, peddler, h Sears
Beach Jesse A, marble cutter, h Ellis
Beach William J, stoker, h Crafton cor Pearl
Beauge A Naomi, school teacher, bds 57 East ave

I couldn't figure out what "bds" meant but what I think it means is that the persons are renting or boarders in that property as opposed to owning it. This directory takes you through the whole town, and while interesting I will just show you the first page. My Sofields were all moved out by this time, and I was really disappointed so I guess that I will never know that exact place where they lived, or whether they moved around town or what.

I have found a few places where my great-grandmother had her shops and of course my great-grandfather worked in the courthouse. Oh yes, also their son James had been a fireman and I know where that building is and he had also worked in the Agitator Newspaper as a teen-ager and that building is now the Deane Center on the corner of Main and Central.

Going back to my trek to town yesterday, I had remembered that I had a date with two ladies from Mahjong to go and see a play at the Warehouse Theatre where I had gone before. I was to meet them in the front at 2PM as it started at 2:30 and we wanted to get good seats. When I got home and looked at the clock it was already 2:22 PM so I rushed out and almost ran to the corner on the next block.

One of the ladies, Lin, didn't show up but the other one, Arline, was already seated and saved me a seat. The play was cute. It was called, *Dancing at Lughnasa.*

The Cast

It took place in Ireland in 1936 and was about five sisters, a brother and their travails. A radio in the play, played music from the 1930s that really made it live to anyone that would have been born in the era. I don't quite understand why it played American music but...oh well, it was a very nice afternoon.

It's Been A Good Week
April 23

I know that I haven't been entering much for you for the last week or so and that is because not much has happened…but now I have a few things to share.

As I have mentioned in previous chapters, I had to be out of this beautiful B&B by May 28th because that is the tourist season and all the rooms in here have reservations starting June 1st. They need the few days to get the place ready.

I have been fretting over this, the whole time because I have so many conditions to fill that I was so afraid one wouldn't be available. I knew that I had a whole month to do this in but I wanted it to be just right. So far this quest of mine has been just right and I didn't want to put a hex on it. Here were my pre-requisites:

1. The home had to be in the Historic District.
2. The rent should be around $850 per month.
3. It had to be furnished.
4. I had to like the furniture.

There is a house one block closer to town then where I am now. Just go one block, turn right and go two houses down. There is a house that I have had my eye on for a long time.

This is the house I've had my eyes on.

Do you remember when I told you before that there was a man that was a contemporary of my great-grandparents named John Bache? Well this house that I had my eye on was the John Bache house. Who is John Bache, you ask? He is the man that went to Gettysburg right after the battle and gathered what today would be considered artifacts, and brought the Wellsboro ones back to their survivors—one of which was Sofield's twisted sword. He gave it to my great-grandmother. I would be living in HIS house!

A historical photograph of the Bache house.

Talk about the historical district! I would be living in another historical house! First there is the one that I am living in now, The Packer House, whereby Nathan Packer and my great-grandfather did real estate transactions together, and they both lived on Main Street…then over to Charles Street where I would be living.

On Easter day, Brian and I walked over there and called the number that was on a For Rent sign in front of the Bache house and I left a message. (I know what you are thinking: "Who calls on real estate signs on Easter?" Desperate people, that's who!)

Well, come Monday this man returned my call and told me that he either rents those apartments for long term or short term because this is a tourist area after June. He said that the apartment that is empty there is spoken for on July 13, 14 and 15, so it wouldn't be available when I needed it and besides that, he wanted $1200 per month for it. Darn!

Then he went on to say that he had another house that was for rent on Pearl Street, the street right behind Main Street. We planned to meet there the next morning at 9:30 AM.

The home on Pearl Street.

As soon as I got there I was a little disappointed for three reasons:

1. It wasn't walking distance to town. Oh, it may be for a younger person but not for me. There were up and down slopes going to and from it.

2. The outside was very boxy looking and it, I found out later, was built in the late 1800s and had the original wood siding on it.

3. It was the last house on the street and the next-door neighbor wasn't very close. I would feel kind of isolated and a little afraid.

I did find out that the price was right: $1000 per month, including all utilities. Oh, another pre-requisite of mine was to have air conditioning and this one did.

The apartment was over to the side of the house and you walked into a long glassed-in porch that was furnished with a nice rocker. The view from that porch is spectacular. Green rolling hills with the crest covered with Pine-type trees. Then you walk inside and *wow*, what a surprise! The furnishings are beautifully done. It has all new furniture, a gas fireplace in the living room, a small bedroom (without much space for clothes) and a second TV.

Then there is a very nice kitchen and a laundry room with washer/dryer and one-and-½ baths. They had done a beautiful job on refurbishing that part of the house. He was working on another part of the house to have another apartment.

This is the barn and rolling hills outside.

I told him that I would take it. We both drove over to my house and I gave him his deposit. I then told him that I would love to be able to see the inside of the Charles Street house so he said, "Let's walk over to it and I'll let you see the inside." I had mentioned before that there is a whole block at the edge of the little town called "The Green" and this house is right across the street from it. I know, in my heart of hearts that my Grandpa Benjamin used to play in this little park as a young boy. He didn't go to the Mansfield Orphan's home until he was about eight. This house is right across a little street from The Green. I had to have it.

When we walked inside, I was surprised at what I saw. When you first walk in there is a long hallway, as if you are in an apartment building with apartment doors on either side. The first room on the left is a little sitting room, very well decorated. There is an overstuffed chair where you would sit and look out at The Green. I wish that I could convey the feelings that I have in that situation but it's hard to. Then you go across the hall and that is the living room, complete with lovely new furniture, a big flat screen TV, et cetera. Then back to the next room across the hall and it is a study with a state of the art glass corner computer desk and chair. Back to the hallway and the next room is the bedroom with a lot more closet space than the one on Pearl Street. In it there was a king-sized bed as opposed to a double bed in the other one. Then across the hallway is a little tiny kitchen with just a hotplate, toaster oven and microwave. No dishwasher, but that's ok. Neither house had a dishwasher. Then on down the hall there are another 1 ½ baths and washer/dryer.

To many people this may not be the type of apartment that they would want because of the hallway situation but for me, it was perfect for two reasons. I know that all of you have heard of the saying: Location, location, location. Well this is one time when that is definitely the case. Not only that, but when Brian comes to stay with me he hates TV and I love it. There's privacy for each individual in this arrangement…but alas, I had taken the other home and this one wouldn't be ready until mid-July, plus it was too expensive. I let the landlord know how much I loved that place and I told him about the John Bache story.

After we got back to my place he said, "Why don't you do this…move to the Pearl Street house for 6 weeks and after the people leave the Charles Street home you can move over there for the same price and I'll help you move. So that is what I did…and by the way, he lowered the rent down to $1000 for me. Pinch me, please.

Do you readers believe this? This man, Joel is his name, was the same dream of a landlord that Nelle has been to me as a landlady. This town is made up of such wonderful loving people—plus the charm of the town itself is indescribable, much as I try. We all have good things happen to us now and then in this life, but the last—I am not sure how far back to go—I will say, couple of years tops them all.

April 24

Thursday Amanda called me and invited me to go to a Mennonite program that they were having at the Presbyterian Church. I gladly accepted the invite as I hadn't been many places lately and I wanted to see the Mennonites all together. As I had explained to Amanda, that I was from California and you never see Mennonites nor Amish in the West and so they are peculiar to Pennsylvania only that if someone saw a woman with those cute little white caps in the supermarket in town in California, for instance, they would be pointed out or photographed.

I remember when Brian first got a job in Chambersburg, Pennsylvania. I was at the post office one day and a Mennonite woman came in there to do business and I whipped out my camera and took a picture of her while she wasn't looking and emailed it back to my family. I can just see them gathering around that picture and wishing they were experiencing my encounter.

I couldn't wait for Friday night to come. Then it came at last. I made sure that my iPad/camera was fully charged because it was going to get used that night! I arrived forty minutes before the show started...that was the plan so that I could take some pictures and talk to the girls in their little white caps. As you will see from the pictures, they were all co-operative.

Sweet Innocence

They were beautiful girls. Not one sign of make-up, just pure innocent beauty. They don't wear jewelry of any kind, not even wedding rings. Their skin is clean, I suppose from not wearing make-up. They have a glow about them. Then as time went on they all started streaming in.

That church, and it is a large church, was practically filled to the brim. The people came from many different congregations and as I looked around I saw a mass of white hats. The men don't dress like the Amish men, insofar as they don't have the beards and they don't just dress in black, just regular nice and neat street wear. Boy, do I sound like a Californian now!!

Next thing I knew there was a tap on my shoulder and it was a man who introduced himself to me as Amanda's father. I immediately saw where Amanda got her sweet and friendly personality as both her parents are like that.

"You are Audrey, aren't you?" he asked.

"Yes, how do you know me?" I replied.

He said that he was Amanda's dad and that she had described me and told him that I would be there. I wonder if it is the fact that I was the only woman in there that was wearing long pants, mascara and dangling earrings. Hmmm.

Amanda and her mom

Then I saw her mom, the one who had done some sewing for me. They started introducing me around to other ladies and I felt so welcome. I wasn't sure how I would be accepted as sometimes you get the idea that they are, what I presume to be, like the Amish, who are more clannish. I hope that I am not being presumptuous about the Amish, but maybe I am.

The program was all music and mostly by children. I was totally amazed that for one solid hour these little children had learned all the words to long songs and also they recited stories in unison, long stories, word for word with no mistakes! Unbelievable!! After that we all talked to each other and I met many very nice and friendly women. We then followed the smell of coffee and made our way downstairs to the kitchen area.

Little Mennonite Choir

I did find out one thing about the Mennonites: they love to cook. I have been watching my weight lately but that was a little more than I could take. I had a very unique veggie pizza made by Amanda's mom. It had Philadelphia Cream Cheese mixed with sour cream as a base with raw veggies on top of a crust. Wow!

April 26

Went to Mahjong today at noon and had a good day with a lot of fun ladies. I only Mahjonged once! Afterward, since I hadn't eaten lunch and it was 4PM, June and I went over to the hospital cafeteria and had dinner. She used to be an RN there but is now retired. The food was great and cheap. We sat and talked for quite a while, while I told her of my ancestors. Probably bored her to tears.

On the way home I decided to take a little ride up Pearl Street to visit the house where I will be living in a month. It was about 6PM and it was absolutely beautiful…the scenery that is. There was a little breeze and it was somewhat chilly out. There were big, white billowy clouds in the otherwise blue sky. The rolling hills were getting very green. As I looked further up on the hill I could see between some trees on the crest that there is a cemetery up there so I got in the car and rode up there and, wow, what beautiful views. Now I am thinking twice about moving to Charles Street. I like them both.

My New Address
April 29

The book that I referred to on page 269, *Life In Wellsboro from 1880-1920* by Gale Largey, shows pictures of homes—inside and outside—from that day and also of the little town as it looked back then. When I purchased the book, it had been out of print so very long that I had to pay $112 for it. I did it gladly.

When I received it, the book had a soft cover and was kind of falling apart at the seams. The pages were in good repair but the cover was separating from the inside and pages were coming loose. I ran over to the library and asked them if they had a lead on a book binding company and they gave me a company called Mechling Bookbindery in Chicora, Pennsylvania. I called them and arranged to send the book to them. I had a hard cover put on and had I them glue the picture on the front of the existing cover glued to the hard cover. That would cost another $50.00 but it was worth it to me. They did a beautiful job.

Inside this book, other than the pictures, are pages of what today would resemble a telephone book. I am including here a scanned picture of one of these pages (see next few pages). Please take note of where I have the arrows pointing.

That is the house owned by John Bache back in the 1890s. He actually had it built before that but that is when the picture was taken. The address was (and is) 4 Charles Street. That is the house that I am moving into in July and it has the same address!

Again, he is the man that brought the twisted sword found on my great-grandfather's body and brought it back to my great-grandmother. There are things about the inside of that house that could be more desired but the fact that I am here mainly because of the history of Wellsboro that relates to my ancestors, the little things that don't suit my fancy are not important. Now I can sit and look out the front window and see "The Green" and picture my grandpa, Benjamin Sofield, playing on there when he was little.

From the Wellsboro Borough Directory, 1899:

EXPLANATIONS

Directory is arranged as follows: 1st, name of individual or firm; 2d, post office address in parenthesis, if different from the name of the town; 3d, the figures following the letter r indicate the number of the road on which the party resides and will be found by reference to the map in the back part of this work; where no road number is given, the party is supposed to reside in the village; 4th, business or occupation; 5th, figures placed after the occupation of a farmer indicate the number of acres owned or leased; 6th, names in bold type are those who have kindly given their patronage to the work and without whose aid its publication would have been impossible.

ABBREVIATIONS — Adv., advertisement; asst., assistant; ave., avenue; bds., boards; bldg., building; cor., corner; Co., company; do., ditto; E., east; h., house; ins., insurance; manuf., manufacturer; mfg., manufacturing; n., near; N., north; pres., president; R. R., railroad; Ry., railway; S., south; W., west; com. trav., commercial traveler; emp., employee.

Adams Nettie (Mrs Walter C) cigarmaker, h 75 Main
Adams Walter C, brakeman F B Ry, bds Coles House
Aker Francis E, glass blower, h 39 East ave
Albert Henry V, meat cutter Fischler Bros, h over 96 Main
Alexander C Austin, engineer F B Ry, h Jackson
Alexander Harriet A, dressmaker Jackson, h do
Alexander Sophia C, widow John, h Jackson
Allen Edward, carpenter, h Pearl
Allen Elizabeth C, widow Thomas, h 24 East ave
Allen William D, (Spencer & Allen) h Crafton
Allington Isaac, teamster, h Nichols cor Sears
American Express Co, A A Truman agt, 65 Main
Andrews Alfred A, glass blower, h Austin
Andrews Francis S, carpenter and farmer 14, h Kelsey
Andrews Laura M, school teacher, bds Cone
Andrews William R, glass blower, h Cone
Arey Sarah, widow Wiliam R, h East ave
Atherton Gilbert C, teamster, h Austin
Atherton Marvin W, laborer, h Austin
Austin Benjamin F, farmer, leases of Robert R Austin 110, h Central ave n boro line
AUSTIN M G & CO (Milo G A and Mrs Charlotte S. Coles) groceries, fruits, provisions, crockery, lamps, glassware, &c 90 Main
AUSTIN MILO G (M G A & Co) h 47 Central ave
AUSTIN ROBERT G manager M G Austin & Co, 90 Main, h 53 Central ave
Austin Robert H, school teacher, bds 25 Grant
Austin Robert R, farmer 110, h 25 Grant

74

Avery Cyrus W, farmer 80, h Kelsey
Avery Jeannette Mrs, h Queen
Avery William O, teamster, h 37 Water
Babcock Charles L, registrar and recorder county office bldg,
 Main, h Walnut
→ Bache John N, real estate, h 4 Charles ←
Bache William, h 55 Pearl
BACHE WILLIAM JR (Nichols & Bache) h 37 Main
Bacon Leon, emp cider mill, bds 23 Conway
BACON MORGAN L SR, physician and surgeon, health
 officer, graduate Long Island College, Main n Queen, h do
BACON M LOUIS JR, physician and surgeon, eye specialist,
 graduate University of Buffalo, Main n Queen, h do
Bacon Oliver, farmer in Delmar 390, h Morris cor Bacon
BACON SETH, propr Wellsboro cider and vinegar works,
 Purple cor Cone, h 23 Conway
Bailey Arthur L, law student, bds, 69 Pearl
Bailey Frank W, clerk 37 Main, bds Austin
Bailey Harry F, school teacher, bds 69 Pearl
BAILEY & HOWE (Ransom W B & Morris D H) dealers in
 wagons, harness, agricultural implements, fertilizers, etc,
 12-16 Waln
Bailey Llellyn L, life and accident insurance and real estate
 and farmer 120, Central ave, h 69 Pearl
BAILEY MYRON F, furniture and undertaking, wagons, har-
 ness and farm implements, first class livery, owner of
 stock farm, 75, in Charleston, breeder and dealer in
 thoroughbred Jersey cattle and dealer in horses, sheep,
 etc, 37 Main, h Austin
BAILEY RANSOM W (B & Howe), 10 cows, farmer, 125, in
 Charleston, h Charleston cor McInroy
Bailey Wallace J, agt Osborn Machine Co, stock dealer, h
 East ave n limits
Baker Carrie L Mrs, domestic, 32 West ave
Baker Edward, farmer, h Bodine
Baker Frank, farmer, 53, h Bodine
Baker Frank L, glass packer, farmer, 24, h Bodine
Baker Joseph C, farmer on shares for L L Bailey, 123, h
 Bailey Lane
Baker Thomas S, painter and paper hanger, h Bodine
Baker William S, painter, bds Bodine
BARNES AUGUSTUS F (B & Roy) h Charleston
BARNES & ROY (Augustus F B & Arthur M R) publishers
 and props The Wellsboro Agitator and job printers, 104
 Main
Barnum Grace B, dressmaker, bds Fellows ave
Barnum Julia, widow Abram, h Fellows ave
Bastian Katharine, widow Samuel, dressmaker, h Water
Battner Matthew, h Tioga
Beach James, peddler, h Sears
Beach Jesse A, marble cutter, h Ellis
Beach William J, stoker, h Crafton cor Pearl
Beauge A Naomi, school teacher, bds 57 East ave

You know it's hard to imagine your heavily mustached grandpa with the skinny legs and grumpy demeanor playing on "The Green" but I am sure that it did happen and I am going to enjoy picturing it. "The

Green" is the cornerstone of Wellsboro as it is the first improvement that was made on Wellsboro property.

Well today is Mahjong and, as usual, I look forward to the nice association of mostly women. Sometimes there will be a man that plays too but the camaraderie that includes a lot of laughter is worth more than the game. I treasure the friends that I have made in this town and hope that I never do anything that jeopardizes those friendships.

I purchased a new Mahjong set and love it. The tiles are real thick and easy to pick up...*now* I'm more popular!

I have been going to Facebook and getting on Gettysburg and Civil War sites and, wow, some of these photographer's sites are like going to an art show. Greg Ainsworth has a site on there that shows his artistry and it's so interesting. He takes these old pictures that had been taken mostly by Matthew Brady and he zeroes in on details that most of our eyes don't catch. You'd be surprised what he finds in those pictures.

When looking at some of the gruesome pictures of the dead men and horses it reminds me of what my great-grandfather and other men from Wellsboro left when they went to war. They left Wynken, Blynken and Nod, The Green, good jobs, wives and children and parents and friends, to dodging bullets and cannon balls, seeing their comrades killed in front of their eyes and then, as in Alfred Sofield's case, their own demise.

I may be prejudice, but to me the Civil War was the worst war that Americans have ever fought. I think the reason is because brothers and friends were fighting each other. I feel that there was more of innocence in those days that we today don't have because of the media. They all depended on each other more back then as they had to in order to survive. I feel that there was less *me, me, me* back then. Maybe I am being naïve in feeling that way. Maybe I am romanticizing those times too much but I really don't think so. How many of us know our neighbors now? I am guilty, I don't. I think that it is because we don't need each other like we did back then.

You remember when, a few chapters ago, I had written to the people that own the house with the red door? Well, I haven't heard back from them to this day. I was hoping that it was because they had been out of town but I see cars coming and going over there sometimes. Many people just want to be left alone. That's their prerogative, but also kind of proves my point. Today we can fend for ourselves more.

I think that by my being here in Wellsboro, those past days seem more real to me. Most people here are friendly. When you walk up the street, people smile and say, "hello." Not everywhere is like that and not everyone is like that. OK, so much for philosophizing and on with the day!

A Statue and Poem
April 30

Winkin, Blynkin and Nod (my house in the background)

When Brian and I came here the second time to
look around this little burg, we stayed at the B&B that is
next door to where I live now on Charles Street. It's called
"Inn on The Green." It really adorable. There are three
bedrooms, each named Winken, Blynkin or Nod. We
stayed in Winken. Cute idea.

The innocence of this little town is caught up in
the fountain which is on The Green: The actual poem is
on a plaque in front of the fountain. I love to study the
looks on the faces of the three children. The little girl,
being the oldest seems to be leading her two siblings,
both, it seems, who are little boys. Since they are in the
open sea she has a look on her face seemingly saying, "I've
got everything under control." She has her hands wrapped
under the chin of her little brother who is in front of her
and sleeping while she looks straight ahead. The other
sibling is behind her just holding on for dear life. It is a
statue to be studied.

> *Wynken, Blynken, and Nod one night*
> *Sailed off in a wooden shoe —*
> *Sailed on a river of crystal light,*
> *Into a sea of dew.*
> *"Where are you going, and what do you wish?"*
> *The old moon asked the three.*
> *"We have come to fish for the herring fish*
> *That live in this beautiful sea;*
> *Nets of silver and gold have we!"*
> *Said Wynken, Blynken, and Nod.*

The old moon laughed and sang a song,
As they rocked in the wooden shoe,
And the wind that sped them all night long
Ruffled the waves of dew.
The little stars were the herring fish
That lived in that beautiful sea —
"Now cast your nets wherever you wish —
Never afeard are we";
So cried the stars to the fishermen three:
Wynken, Blynken, and Nod.

All night long their nets they threw
To the stars in the twinkling foam —
Then down from the skies came the wooden shoe,
Bringing the fishermen home;
'Twas all so pretty a sail it seemed
As if it could not be,
And some folks thought 'twas a dream they'd dreamed
Of sailing that beautiful sea —
But I shall name you the fishermen three:
Wynken, Blynken, and Nod.

Wynken and Blynken are two little eyes,
And Nod is a little head,
And the wooden shoe that sailed the skies
Is a wee one's trundle-bed.
So shut your eyes while mother sings
Of wonderful sights that be,
And you shall see the beautiful things
As you rock in the misty sea,
Where the old shoe rocked the fishermen three:
Wynken, Blynken, and Nod.

Who Would've Known?
April 30

Since it's raining pretty hard today I decided that I wouldn't be going anywhere…so I decided to visit my kids and grandkids on Facebook. (No wonder the post office is going broke) I have garnered quite a few "friends" on Facebook from Gettysburg, who are interested in the Civil War and especially those photographers that take such beautiful pictures. The Gettysburg Battlefield is gorgeous as it stands but when the camera bugs get out there and know what they are doing, it's breathtaking.

Today while looking at some of my Facebook Gettysburg buddies I came across a man that was a link to a friend that I had been following. His name is AJ Freeze. I went to Mr. Freeze's Facebook site and started looking around and noticed that he had a little collage of pictures of Gettysburg soldiers that had been killed there. He had

it on slides with music playing. Right away I thought, I
wish that I had something like that with my great-
grandfather's picture on it along with some related
pictures, maybe of Wellsboro and some of the McPherson
Barn where he was killed. After thinking about it for a
while I asked him if he would do me that favor and he
agreed.

He asked me to send him about 7 pictures and I
started sending them. Then he asked me who my great-
grandfather was and I told him. Then he asked me if he
was a Bucktail and when I said that he had been the
Captain of the 149th Company A, a Bucktail he wrote
back: Oh my, I owe you this one My ancestor was with
the troops that bore down on the Bucktails at McPhersons
Ridge. My ancestor may have been the one that "pulled
the trigger, as it were." Then he said, "Ok, saved that one.
Send the others along. I will work on something for you
today. It will be my honor to do this for you considering
our odd historic relation."

He said that the name of those troops were the
Brockenbroughs brigade from South Carolina. Maybe the
troops mixed in with the South Carolinans, I don't know.
Needless to say I was in shock. When Leslie and Brian
and I took the tour in Gettysburg a few years ago that is
when we found out exactly where he died. Then later that
year when I was hired for a short time from Brian's
company to work in the Gettysburg Courthouse I would
drive over the very street where he had been struck down.
Sometimes I would get out of the car and walk over to the
McPherson Barn. I would look up at Herr's Ridge and
wonder who it was that had done this. I even asked Rich

Kohr that question when taking the tour but he didn't'
seem to want to answer me.

I knew that they were Robert E Lee's troops but
which state did they come from and who was the
overseeing general. Rich has probably run in to people
who still hold an angry grudge and who, maybe, would do
something about it so he just didn't want to take any
chances. Later I started looking for the name of the
general in charge of the Confederates that day that were
on Herr's Ridge and it was General Heth from Virginia.

I will tell you the truth, when AJ Freeze told me
this, I got tears in my eyes and found it almost hard to
believe that I have come full circle on this quest. Even
though it wasn't Mr. Freeze's fault, he didn't do it, he is so
contrite about the whole thing that I have to shake it off.
When the re-enactors get together and do what they do,
they all seem to get along and show respect to each other.
When that war ended and before Lincoln was so brutally
murdered, he had the band play Dixie and referred to the
Southerners as his brothers, with "no malice." Now for
those that still feel the same way that they felt back then,
that is, they believed that slavery should continue or just
let itself "run out" so to speak, then I can't help but feel
more than irked at their attitude but in the places that I
have lived I don't run into those kinds of people.

I have invited Mr. Freeze to come to the Bucktail
Reunion and maybe we can talk to the group there about
our findings. That would be a good story.

Editor's Note: AJ Freeze wrote later that he had done some more research and he surmises that it may not have been his ancestor who "pulled the trigger."

Genealogy-Bank Interesting
May 1

I know that this book is starting to sound like a book of advertisements but when I include a business that I am pleased with, I really mean it. If there are any of you out there that either is doing their genealogy or maybe just interested in reading old newspapers, especially ones from where your ancestors or even you lived in the past, go to genealogybank.com. I found some very interesting things about my Sofield history in Wellsboro.

There are a couple of them that I would like to share with you because it makes an interesting read. My great-grandfather and his dad had a business as partners in the 1840s. His dad, John Sofield, had been a tinner and I can see that he wanted his sons to follow in his footsteps. You can see in this ad that they were selling stoves.

Then I find in later ads that he added another son, William, and a few months later his name was removed from the ad and AJ Sofield was again included. I, at first, thought that maybe William wasn't good at the trade, but learned later that he went off to Illinois and opened his own business in Monmouth, Illinois, and whose house I have been in (that will be a later chapter). Evidently, AJ Sofield didn't adhere to the tin or stove business because he later, it shows, was trying to get into politics. I found an article in 1849 where he was a member of the Democratic Party and actually a chairman and part of a committee. In this article it lists the different articles of faith, as it were, that they were committed to. Here is one of them that really made me feel good.

Thomas Jefferson's Decree
The Northwest Ordinance, officially titled "An Ordinance for the Government of the Territory of the United States North West of the River Ohio," was adopted by the Confederation Congress on July 13, 1787. Also known as the Ordinance of 1787, the Northwest Ordinance established a government for the Northwest Territory, outlined the process for admitting a new state to the Union, and guaranteed that newly created states would be equal to the original thirteen states. Considered one of the most important legislative acts of the Confederation Congress, the Northwest Ordinance also protected civil liberties and outlawed slavery in the new territories.

The subject of slavery in reference to my great-grandfather has been of great importance to me. I know that Wellsboro was very much against it, to the degree that one of the judges here actually hired two run-away slaves and when the bounty hunters came looking for them, they were hidden.

Also when Lincoln gave a speech in mid-1862 saying that slavery in the secession states would be freed, as I have mentioned before, many prejudiced Union Soldiers walked off the battlefields, saying that they wouldn't fight for the N----r. The actual freedom didn't come into effect until January 1, 1863, and Captain Sofield stayed on.

Now that fits in with the article in this newspaper, showing that he was not only against the spread of slavery but also in the article it shows that they were putting a stop to taking property away from the destitute. He's a hard one to psychoanalyze. I think that I have him pegged as rather a cool (not cold, but cool) blooded man, not very interested in his family but more interested in climbing the ladder of success in politics, but when I see what kind of politics he was interested in I have to give it another thought. We are all a conglomeration of leanings and prejudices and softness and hardness so I guess he fits that picture that we all fit in. I do see that he was ambitious and maybe to a fault. His son, my grandpa wasn't like that and neither was my dad nor his brother, Roye...but their sister, Helen, was as I have touched on previously.

In the next chapter I will talk about my experience in Monmouth, Illinois, and visiting my great-granduncle John B. Sofield's house that is still standing and occupied.

The Haunted House
May 3

Doug Rankin's home was built in 1882 by a local hardware salesman who lived there for a few years until Chancey Hardin moved in. Hardin was a fairly well known banker in Monmouth. He lived in the house for a while until the Hunter sisters moved in. They were five sisters who lived in the house for 60 years, essentially as spinsters.

The common belief regarding this house is that it is haunted. This from the Peoria Paranormal Society:

> Rankin, professor of theater at Monmouth College, moved into the house in 1986. Since then, some strange things have happened in the house, according to Rankin. Interesting things such as: guests of the house feeling sensations like being grabbed or touched, lights turning on and off by themselves and perhaps most to Rankin's

annoyance, disappearing items. "In more recent years, we'd find things moving by themselves that would later turn up in the dryer," Rankin said. "Everything from a cellphone to sunglasses." Chris Fleming, who co-hosted the television show "Dead Famous," was the first paranormal investigator to check out Rankin's house. He was on campus and Rankin invited him over on a whim to continue his haunted tour. "We had 20 or so students with us in the living room, around a lit candle," Rankin said. According to Rankin, Fleming was taunting and antagonizing the "spirits" of the house, when, "We saw the candle flame shoot straight up to the ceiling," Rankin said. Rankin's home was the PPS's last stop in Monmouth. Unusual things happened when the group arrived outside Rankin's home on Broadway. "The medium looked up at a window in the house and said, 'That's where it all happened,'" Rankin said. "She was right." Rankin still doesn't know why, but there has been a lot of unusual activity in that room. Waldschmidt and Rankin's wife used dowsing — or divining — rods to communicate with the spirits of the house. Rods are extended and the spirits move them when asked a question: left for "yes," and right for "no." The ghost box also picked up responses in Rankin's home, Waldshmidt said. "It's strange to talk about, because there's no proof," Rankin said. "We've had a lot of interesting things happen over the years, and more than a few people who had no knowledge of it experienced it."

Bravo!
The Pet of the Nine

Sofield & Schussler.
Monmouth. Ill.

The house was built by my great-granduncle, John B. Sofield. He wasn't merely a local hardware salesman, he owned the local Tinning/Stove Company, and, as you will see from his ad, he was quite the entrepreneur.

I see that he also had a good sense of humor. I like that. His wife, Helen's, obituary tells of their travels and how they landed in Monmouth:

Mrs. Helen M. Sofield was born in Lenox, Madison County, New York, December 8, 1837. Most of her girlhood days were spent there, but as early as 1857 she moved with her parents to Osawatomie, Kansas, where she met Mr. J. B. Sofield. They were united in marriage in Galesburg, Illinois, October 19, 1859, and returned to Oswatomie and remained a year. They then moved to Kirkwood, Illinois, and lived 21 years. Both united with the Universalist church there of which Mrs. Sofield was a trusted member when she died. During the war Mrs. Sofield was busily engaged in the sanitary commission working with Mary A. LIVERMORE. She was always a diligent worker with any society that helped the poor and needy. Mr. and Mrs. Sofield moved to Monmouth, Illinois, from Kirkwood, lived there six years and came to Washington in 1886.

Until two years ago Mrs. Sofield has had quite good health, but then she was troubled with dropsy and heart failure. Her last two years have been years of suffering. She knew her time must soon come, and was ready and willing to go. There were born to Mr. and Mrs. Sofield, five girls, four died under the age of nine years and were buried in Kirkwood, Illinois.

Back to the haunted house and my personal experiences in it. In 2008 my daughter, Leslie and her granddaughter, Kyra, who was eleven at the time, and I took a very fun vacation. We were to go to Springfield, Illinois, first because I had a friend that I had done real estate with when I lived in Auburn, California, and her husband lived in Springfield. She had invited me to come and visit her sometime in the past and I thought that this would be a perfect opportunity. After all, that is where Lincoln lived and is buried. There was also a new Lincoln Museum there that I was dying to see. Of course I so wanted to see and walk through his house. It would be perfect. After our stay there we were going to take the train to New York and Washington DC and Gettysburg. What a trip that was. I'll never forget how wonderful it was to show my great-granddaughter the history that applied to her, too. We called it our History Trip.

We arrived in Springfield and my friend and her husband picked us up at the train station and we drove to their very comfortable and cozy home. While there we did everything that we had planned on doing. We walked through Lincoln's home and saw the kitchen where Mary Todd Lincoln did all her cooking. It is a tiny kitchen but it was supposed to have been pretty much now as it was then. Then we went to his mausoleum and it was grandiose. There were beautiful bronze statues of him everywhere. As a side note: I have a relative (distant) buried right outside of Lincoln's burial site. If any of you readers are Lincoln enthusiasts and you find yourself in Springfield, Illinois, please go to the Lincoln Museum, as it is so interesting. It's the most creative museum that I have ever been to.

Before I left home to go on my trip I had called my cousin, David Finney, in Omaha, Nebraska, the same cousin that initially got me on this quest and whom this book is dedicated to. I told him of my plans and *Wow!* am I glad that I did. He started telling me about our great-granduncle John B. Sofield and the house that he had built in Monmouth, Illinois.

David said that when he had found out about it and had done some research, he contacted the people who live in it now and surprisingly they had already done what we today call a title search on it, but to me it was, the genealogy of that home, a Sofield home. He gave me their phone number and excitedly insisted that I go see them if at all possible.

It was a Sunday afternoon that I called their house and she, Tami Rankin, answered the phone. I asked to speak to Doug Rankin and she told me that he was busy at the moment but could she take a message. I told her that I was a Sofield and that I was going to be in Springfield in the next week or so and that David, my cousin, had told me to call. She immediately told me that she would get Doug to the phone.

She went on to explain that every Sunday while in season, Doug watched the games on TV and she was instructed never to call him away from the phone, but she knew that he would be very anxious and interested to speak to me. When he came to the phone it was as if we knew each other. We talked Sofield as if he were one. It was very plain that he was as interested in our family as we were.

I told Doug that I would try to talk my friends into taking us to see them. They lived about 140 miles from Monmouth but I had a plan and a determination to get there. Now this was before we even made the trip. This phone call occurred when I was still in California, so it was on my mind the whole time...I knew that I had to pick the right timing while we were in Springfield to ask the friend to take us there and at the time, I had never even met him, only her.

Once we arrived and got settled in the house and that they had taken us to all the local places that I mentioned before, (we were going to stay there three nights and four days) my friend's husband asked me what I wanted to do that day. They had already taken me to the museum; the mausoleum and Lincoln's house so I guess it seemed to him that I had seen all I had wanted to see. Not quite! I told him the Monmouth story and about that house. Also my Dad had been born in Galesburg, Illinois, and I wanted to see that, too...so I said to him, "If I give you $100 to go towards gas and your trouble and pay for your lunch, would you mind if we take a trip today to

Monmouth and then to swing back through Galesburg
before heading home?" I wanted to go to the Galesburg
Courthouse and see if they have any records of where my
grandparents had lived when my dad was born. He
immediately said, "Let's go!!!"

I was so excited. We all got ready and I called the
Rankins and told them about what time we'd be there and
she said that Doug had to work and she had a guitar
lesson to give that day but that she would cancel it and to
come on over.

It took us about three hours to get there and then
we pulled up to 608 E. Broadway Street. I had seen the
picture that you are seeing now and I was a little a nerved
to see it in person, but the friendly greeting that we got
from Tami when we pulled up along with the hugs and
handshakes and the welcome she gave our friends
overcame any nerves that I had.

When we walked up the front steps to go into the foyer I started doing what I do here in Wellsboro, and that is, picturing my descendent standing on this porch and looking out at the other mansions in the neighborhood. That is really true, that part of E. Broadway has some beautiful mansions that are as old as this one is, all refurbished to reflect the modern touches of today.

Once we entered the foyer and turned right to go into the parlor, as they called it back then, there was a full sized manikin of a butler standing inside the parlor's entrance holding a tray. Naturally, I jumped a mile. He was very lifelike. As for the décor, they chose to keep it as if it were new in the late 1800s. The pictures on the walls were in the old oval metal frames and there was a picture of what they were told was a Sofield that someone had found in a town where the lady in the picture had lived. I wish that now I remembered who that lady was supposed to have been as I have done so much more research since that time.

We were then led into the next room that was the dining room. It had a long banquet table, you know, the kind where the head of the house sits on one end and the little lady sits on the other end and the children and or guests line up on either side. It was there that we sat down and ate the hors d'oeuvres that she had so hospitably prepared for us. You must remember there were five of us there. As we sat down and got acquainted that's when the ghost stories started coming out, but not before she called her husband, Doug, to try to come home from work for a short period to meet us. As you can see from the first of this paragraph, he is a professor of theater in the nearby Monmouth College and as hard as it was to get away, he came home.

One of the stories that she told was the one at the opening of this chapter and as we talked we could see that the previously friendly ghosts or spirits or whatever it was in there didn't like to be mocked. They told us that every Halloween they have an open house because all the young people around have heard these stories and they want to see for themselves.

Doug said that when his parents came to spend a few nights with them that they left the next day because of eerie things that were happening in the house. Their dog would bark at the heat register on the floor for no apparent reason…but the creepiest thing that I remember her telling us about was that one day she was upstairs on the landing just outside the bedroom. She was hanging a picture on the wall and *something* put its hands on her shoulder. She said that it was gentle but frightening and she turned around real quickly and sternly demanded that they didn't touch her again. The hands immediately dropped and it never happened again, at least up to that time.

She then took us to the whole tour and the house was very fashionable for that time and the Rankins are still working on doing more. She also took us outside and showed us her garden and other improvements that they had made on the house.

I emailed Doug the other day and he is going to send me an update of what they have been doing with it since we were there. I really believe that they are there to stay. I feel that they are part of the Sofield clan as they are so loyal to the name. I remember one day a few years ago

I found on the Internet where there was a Sofield and a Rankin in business together in Monmouth in the 1800s. At the moment I don't remember what type of business that it was and when I sent them the information he was more interested in the part that Sofield played in the business than he was in the Rankins. Now that's loyalty!

For those of you who use a computer and in order to see the inside of the house please go to this website: *http://rankindesigns.com/house/photoindex.htm*. It is very interesting!

On the drive back we were all talking a mile a minute about what we had just experienced. Then it was off to Galesburg. Galesburg is only twenty miles from Monmouth and that is the town where my grandmother was born and where she and my grandfather Benjamin were married. I have their original marriage certificate. Once we were in Galesburg, a clean little town, we stopped for lunch at a nice little sandwich shop that dealt with healthy nosh. Then we went to the courthouse to see what I could find.

The same courthouse my dad saw.

We went inside and I asked if I could have Alfred Jay Sofield's birth certificate and they looked and couldn't find it. I knew that he was born there and I insisted that it had to be there somewhere.

After a while they asked me if he had been in the military and I said, "Yes, he was in WWI, but that he had enlisted in Los Angeles, California. Then they knew just where to go. They found it and luckily for me, their home address was on the certificate. We immediately drove over to that address and lo and behold it was a corner lot...and I do mean a lot as there was no building on it. It was next door to an old and beautiful stone church and the cornerstone indicated that it had been there when my grandparents lived there. I took pictures that I have since lost or misplaced. Then we departed and headed back to Springfield. What a wonderful experience that trip had been. My study of genealogy had led me to the history of the paternal side of my family that not too many people get to experience.

It's been wonderful...and it's not over.

An Even Better Week!
June 20

At this point I want to refer you back to the chapter dated April 23, 2014, called "It's Been A Good Week." Well, I still can't believe it, but the next couple of weeks were even better.

My phone rang recently and it was Joel Young who owns the house on Charles Street telling me that the people living upstairs in that house put in their thirty-day notice. He asked, that if I didn't mind climbing stairs, would I be interested in looking at it? WOULD I EVER!! Luckily for me Brian was here that day. Both he and I met Joel over on Charles Street and we walked upstairs: it was perfect. I was walking along the hallway looking in each room and Brian was ahead of me and he came to the living room and called out, "This is perfect, we'll take it." When I got to the living room I could very well see why, it

314 | Audrey Sofield Barber

is huge. It's about 30X18' and as you look out the window you get a great view of The Green.

As I write this, it is June 10. We have lived in it now since May 22, and I am loving it. As I sit at my computer I turn my head to the right and look at all the activities going on over at The Green…or on a calm day, I just stare at that little fountain with the statue of Wynkin, Blynkin and Nod and I have to pinch myself to see if it is real. I've never been so happy.

On June 20-June 22, we had the Laural Festival here in Wellsboro. That is something that I have been hearing about ever since I moved here about six months ago. Little did I know that I could experience a lot of it without having to leave my front room. The first thing that happened was on June 20 I heard some drums outside. When I looked out my window, I saw a semi-circle of chairs that had been set up in front of some band players that were getting ready to perform. At that point I raced down with my lawn chair and set myself up in the front row and the people started pouring in. In no time at all there was standing room only. I've never seen a town that is so interested in the culture that is presented to them like I've seen here.

The band was called The Town Band made up of people of all ages starting with; it looked like, high school students to men and women with gray hair. They featured marching music, which happens to be one of my favorites of all-time. I took some good videos of it and have played it over and over since coming home. Now here is the funny part (with me there's always a funny part)…the next day it was announced that Saturday afternoon there was going to be a men and women's choir that was to be held at the Presbyterian Church. I was anxious to see it and take some pictures and videos of the music. When I entered the church there was standing room only but I nuzzled my way in to a seat down towards the front and as I pulled out my video iPad to get a good shot of the singers, I pressed the "take a video button" and lo and behold the marching band was playing loudly from my camera and this is while the choir was singing! OH. MY. GOSH. I scrambled to turn it off and tried to start it again without the band but lo and behold: more marching music! Every head in the place turned to look at my fumbling around. Have I mentioned that I have a love/hate relationship with electronics? If not, I'm mentioning it now.

Now let me mention another embarrassing event coming from, this time, Brian! Sunday, the last venue of the Laurel Festival, there was an interdenominational church service held on The Green. There were many chairs that were filled and there was music and singing that filled the air. Such a nice atmosphere until Brian decided to take his car and back out of our driveway and take a ride. This car is new to us and he isn't familiar with the alarm system. (I think that you know where this is headed.) He stuck the key in the lock and right about the time they were singing Amazing Grace, our alarm system was accompanying it with *Beep Beep Beep Beep*--or should I say *Blast! Blast! Blast!* You have all heard how loud car alarms are and, of course, when you don't know your new car that well you are scrambling and making a fool of yourself to get it shut off.

For those of you who have never been to Wellsboro and seen the geographical relationship that our house has to The Green, you can't really get the full benefit of the racket that it was creating. The group was playing practically right up to the curb and Charles Street is a little one way street: it's *very* close. To me it lasted forever but in reality it only did about seven or eight loud beeps/blasts.

Now that my thoughts are firmly on interruptions I'll go back to the day of the Town Band. While playing a tune that had a lot of horns, the Episcopalian Church, which is right across the other street from The Green, always acts as the town's Grandfather Clock. Well, it must have been about 4PM because the church chimes, and they are loud, started chiming the little ditty that they chime before counting off the hours. When you play a horn, the way that you can tell if you are in tune or not is by hearing it. Needless to say there were a few horns that were, shall we say, a little off key. The audience was tittering away but I don't think that the band players were.

Saturday was the parade! The song *I Love A Parade* must have been written for me because I most certainly do love a parade. When I was growing up in California my mother never missed a parade that went through Riverside and we would dress for the occasion. If it was honoring cowboys we'd dress like cowboys and I remember when we had De Anza Days (De Anza was a Spaniard who founded Riverside) we dressed in Spanish costumes. Well, this last Saturday's parade seemed to lean pretty much to patriotism and some local themes such as honoring the local Soldiers and Sailors Hospital, the Boy Scouts and some local political figures, along with the Laurel Festival Queen and her princesses. What I have always loved the most, however, are the marching bands—especially

Marine Bands as they have perfect pitch when they play. It was a long parade but not too long; it was just right. The sun was out and I was sitting in it. We were sitting across the street from the Court House and my mind went back to August of 1862 when the Bucktails all gathered out there to say their good-byes to their families. I thought of my great-grandfather marching away, never to be seen by his family again. I may have been standing or sitting on the very same spot as my great-grandmother stood as she waved her good-bye to him. That, to me, is so sad as we never know what tomorrow will bring. I still find it hard to believe that I am surrounded so much by my history.

From Never Never Land to Utopia
June 23

Yesterday, ahh yesterday. There is something that I have been putting off doing simply because I thought that I would get a big yawn from the powers that be at the courthouse. Ever since I arrived here in Wellsboro and I told my story to people as to why I was here and about my ancestors, they always asked, "What was the last name?" When I said Sofield, Scott Gitchell was the only person that showed recognition. From the others I would just get a big "deer in the headlights" look. That, to me, was *so* disappointing. He was so much into this town. He was in every activity, so much that to the point I feel that, that is what he was doing instead of home eating with his family and playing with his boys, thus the letter of apology to his wife in the letter that he had written two weeks before he was killed. I fear I am being redundant, but it all fits into a pattern.

So getting back to what I think that this little town owes to him, I got the idea that I needed to set up some sort of memorial for him. Yesterday, as it turned out, was to be the day of my march to the Wellsboro Court House (although the march is only one half a block). I had with me a great picture of him, one that I had forgotten that I had. It was an 8X10. Don't get me wrong, I only have one picture of him, which was the professional picture that you see on page 31 and the back of the book, but this one I am talking about is large. I carefully put that picture in my bag and went ahead with my agenda.

As with all courthouses today, I had to go through a security system, et cetera. Once that was done I asked the two nice security guards where I could find one of the commissioners. They reminded me that it was 12:30 PM. As usual, I had picked the wrong time to find anyone available there. One of the guards, thankfully, had gotten

on his phone and the next thing I knew a very kindly faced man came out and introduced himself to me as Commissioner Mark Hamilton (left). We sat down right there on a soft, leather-like bench in the entry while I told him my story. I tried to keep it simple—but simple just isn't my style—yet I noticed that he didn't seem bored and was actually showing interest.

Commissioner Hamilton started educating me on the changing of the term "Justice of the Peace" to what they are now called, which is "Magistrates." He also told me that they are like judges, in fact, they are judges. I asked him if they were considered judges back in the 1800s and he said, "yes." That really stunned me. Now I *knew* that my great-grandfather had to be recognized and deserved a memorial. I asked him if the Magistrates judged criminal cases back in the day and he said that he had wondered that too and had read somewhere that when Jefferson had been a Magistrate in Philadelphia (I didn't even know that he had lived in Philadelphia, let alone been a Magistrate there) he was remembered, but not quoted, as saying, "The reason that I am retiring early is because I can't stand the depressing job of judging criminals." That is not a direct quote but is the gist that he was saying. He said that he is going to try to find the article for me. I have done a Google search, and although I didn't find that thought by Jefferson, I got pretty much into reading about him.

Okay, back to the subject at hand. Mr. Hamilton said the he thought that the most appropriate place for Sofield's memorial picture to hang would be in the present Magistrate's office. Wow, I was thrilled beyond thrilled. He excused himself while he took the trouble to go back to his office and come out with the Magistrate's name and phone number. It turned out to be a Mr. Rob Repard, Magistrate in the Department of Justice. This was starting to sound more important by the minute. The first thing that I asked Mr. Hamilton was, "Is he nice and approachable?" He said, "Stern, but nice." Uh oh, stern? Ok, Audrey, turn on the charm, if you have any! Commissioner Hamilton gave me Mr. Repard's phone number and said that the best thing to do was to go and call him after lunch, then he got up and went back to his office. As I got up to leave one of the security guards said, "Mr. Repard wants to see you in his office, and it is right down the hall there." I asked him how Mr. Repard even knew that I was there and he said that he had called him and told him my story and that he was anxious to talk to me. Have any of you ever felt like you were walking two or three inches off the ground? Well that's how I was walking as went down the hall to Mr. Repard's office. The minute I walked in there was a smile that went from ear to ear when he saw me. He acted as thrilled as I was.

Magistrate Rob Repard

He was at his counter assisting some people and when he was through he opened the door to his office and motioned for me to come in. His office was nice and large with a smattering of pictures on the walls. They were mostly scenic pictures but none of past judges or people at all, for that matter. I sat down across from him and started to tell him my story and he was very interested. The more interested he got the more thrilled I got. I pulled out the picture that I brought with me of my great-grandfather and it was then that I told him that Mr. Hamilton thought that if there was any place in the court house that my great-grandfather's picture belonged, it was in Mr. Repard's office and he agreed. Then he stood up and said, "I think I have a better place for it, follow me."

He opened another door and we walked into his courtroom where he presided and there they were, pictures of past judges in very large and substantial frames. He iterated that it was *his* courtroom. Does this mean that AJS had his own courtroom? The two or three inches that I was walking off the floor now began to rise—even though I knew that this wasn't the exact room where the original Justice of the Peace's office was back in the 1800s because the building that we were in was next door to the original courthouse.

He showed me a picture that was behind and to the left of the judge's bench. That was a group picture taken in 1953 of many of the past magistrates, all of whom would be gone by now. That picture was in a less than professional frame and it had, in handwriting below it the names of each past judge. I have a feeling that that is where they will want to put AJS's picture. He said that he just had one person that he had to ask and that was the owner of the building. I'm not sure if that is a committee, a board or a person but in the meantime I am waiting for a phone call.

When I happily left the building I started walking down the street practically singing as I went. I headed to town where I sat on a bench and called one of my daughters. She jokingly (I think) said, "Why don't they name a street after him…no, a statue!" I laughed at that one. I'm just happy that they want a picture in the courtroom.

When I look up at the picture of Mr. Repard I now picture my great-grandfather in a black robe. I had never given it a thought that he was a judge. Now I am going to have to see if I can figure out the difference between a regular presiding judge and a magistrate.

After my conversation on the phone with my daughter, I continued to walk and I heard music from across the street. I looked over and there was a piano on the sidewalk with a girl playing something quite well. I turned around and as I faced front, there was another piano. It was painted in psychedelic colors with the wording on it, PLAY ME I'M YOURS. It seemed that the one song that I can still remember from my limited repertoire was, "The Man I Love" so I looked around to make sure that no one could see me and I sat down and started playing. To complement this Utopian scene, the weather was about 74 degrees with a slight breeze—or should I say, "perfect." We've all had those days where it seems that "this is the way life should be in a Norman Rockwell world" and it was this day.

After I finished the song I was glad when I looked around some more and nobody was in earshot…or so I thought. I was right outside the Citizens Bank and when I finished the song and stood up to leave, all of a sudden the door swung open and a teller stuck her head out and yelled over at me, "We could hear you so we turned the radio off and listened…thank you, we enjoyed it." That was my second thrill for the day. Then I walked into the Fifth Season fancy department store and bought a very nice wooden frame and off I went. I came back home and

anxiously ran upstairs and told Brian what had just
happened and he was happy for me.

Last weekend when I was walking through The
Green during the Laurel Festival, when it had all the
tented vendors in there I had passed a framing tent with
all sorts of different frames on display. I stopped and
talked to him about doing a frame for my great-
grandfather's picture so that I could display it on the table
that we would be using for the authors at the Bucktail
Reunion. I took his card and planned on calling him in a
few days.

Now that I had two places for this picture to go I
got on the phone and called the framer and made an
appointment to go and see him. The next day, Tuesday,
we went over there with the thought that I would have to
buy a frame from him and he would mat and place it in
the frame and that I would use the one that I had
purchased to use in my house, but when I went there and
he saw the frame in my sack he suggested that we use that
frame. It was only an 8x10 frame and I had wanted a
larger one but I saw how he put it together and how nicely
it fit that I left it with him and I am to pick it up next
week. I will use it at the reunion and then take it to the
courthouse at once afterwards.

After I had gone to the courthouse and played the
piano it still wasn't even 10AM, and I was to play Mahjong
at exactly 10AM. After dancing around the house and
telling Brian about everything, I went out and started
walking again over to play Mahjong. Of course I told
them all about my morning and they were thrilled for me.
Then I was handed this sheet of paper from Lin, who is

kind of one of the matriarchs of the group. She formed a
little club called The Mahjong Club and gave each
member a title, of which mine was, Fun Raiser.

THE
MAH AT POP'S
POP'S CULTURE SHOPPE
MAH JONGG CLUB

CONSTITUTION
NATIONAL MAH JONGG LEAGUE, INC.
OFFICIAL STANDARD HANDS AND RULES

MISSION STATEMENT: TO ENJOY MAH JONGG
GOALS: TO HELP NEW PEOPLE LEARN THE GAME
CHARITY: FOSTER CHILDREN

TUESDAYS AT 10:00 AM
SATURDAYS AT NOON

CLUB OFFICERS
PRESIDENT SUSAN STRASSBURG
VICE PRESIDENT TERESA CARUZZO
TREASURER ARLINE BUCHMAN
SECRETARY JUNE TEAGLE
PARLIAMENTARIAN LIN NIBERT
SALPF JULIAN STAM
HOSPITALITY ANJA STAM
LIAISON SHELLY DUNDINWALKER
LIAISON KATHY MCQUAID
PUBLIC RELATIONS SALLY URBAN
FUN RAISER AUDREY MYERS

I couldn't have been more complimented. After
that I walked home very fast and fixed us something to
eat, I went to the little playhouse across the street called
the Warehouse Theatre and saw a little play that one of
my Mahjong friends, Arline, was in. She is moving right
around the corner from me towards the end of July and I
look forward to it.

It is now 3:30 AM and Brian is asleep but I woke up and while it's quiet I had to get this on paper. Now…on to the next day or so.

A Large Setback
July 8

If there was ever something that had bad timing, this was it! On about June 26 I started feeling sick and weak. I went to the doctor and they gave me Sulpha for an infection to be taken for five days. On the fifth day I wasn't feeling much better, in fact, I was feeling worse. It turns out that I was having a reaction to the pills. By evening I was full-blown sick with a temperature and the chills. Brian took me to the Soldiers and Sailors Hospital that is two blocks from home. It ended up that I was in there for five days and nights, from the 30th to the 4th of July. Today is the 8th and I'm still so weak that it is hard to get around. The prognosis?: pneumonia, sepsis and a slight heart attack.

Could it have come at a worse time? The Bucktail Reunion will be here in three weeks and my daughter,

Leslie, and great-granddaughter Kyra will be here on July 30. It was my dream to show them around town and introduce them to my friends, et cetera. When I first got home from the hospital on the 4th, my other daughter, Randa, and her husband, Paul, drove down here from Harriman, New York, and helped me with the necessities around the house. That was so helpful. They would take walks and got acquainted with our cute little town and they, too, were impressed. They stayed for two nights and had to head back home and to work.

I'm trying to catch up in my mind all that I have to do before the reunion. I had my great-grandfather's picture framed so that I can have it sitting on the table where I'm going to give out my booklets and after that, take it to the Magistrates Court Room to have it put on the wall.

During this down time, I've realized how truly great the Civil War re-enactors are so great to us ancestors. This is what I found on Facebook the other day.

•From: Bruce Petro
To: Audrey Barber... Went to see the Captain today after the reenactment.. just had to
LikeLike · · Stop Notifications · Share · *July 6*

Along with that was a picture that he took of AJS's grave.
Then I mentioned that I was sick and I received this message from below. By the way, I have never met nor talked to Michael Parana but this is how we ancestors are treated.

Michael Parana Miss Audrey~~~~ We too send you our well wishes from Clearfield, Huntingdon & Elk Counties~~~of prayers for a speedy recovery. Yours Respectfully, Michael.
23 hours ago · Like

Audrey Barber All your respect and good wishes are like medicine to me. I want to see you on Saturday even if you have to come to my apt. I am right across the street from The

Green at 2 Charles St. Apt. 3.   808.346.7549. Want to see you both.
13 hours ago · Like

Bruce Petro Miss Audrey Barber it will be very late Saturday night when we would arrive perhaps Sunday?
9 hours ago · Like

Audrey Barber Sunday's good!
6 hours ago · Like · 1

Bruce Petro We will be in touch thank you
6 hours ago · Like

These men have a genuine love for the men and their families who were Union Soldiers. They are so respectful, I assume, the way they were in the 1800s. It warms one's heart.

As I stare out the window at the beautiful Green, I so want my life back. Maybe I'm being melodramatic but I miss that I can't go out and take a walk and go over and visit with my friend Toni Smith who owns "Natural Ways." Or stop in and say, "hi" to Kasey at the book store then swing around the corner to and say "hi" to Anja and Julian at Pops Culture, my Mahjong hangout...all the while seeing people that I am acquainted with while walking down the street, or stopping and playing a tune on the one of the little pianos that they have in sundry places on Main St. To me, this is a storybook town and I can now, for a time, only look at it from my window.

Time For Reflections
July 11

Well, here it is three weeks before the Bucktail
Reunion and I still am so weak from this pneumonia that I
wonder if I'll be able to take part in the celebration. Leslie
and Kyra will be here to help, but there are things that I
need to do to prepare for the reunion and they will only
be here one day and a half before everything starts. I
guess this is the other shoe that I have been waiting to
drop…currently dropping.

I know, it could have been a lot worse, but I just
hate to see my happy time in this town being disturbed by
anything. I miss going for walks, visiting my friends,
playing Mahjong, and most of all, I miss my energy. My
doctor told me yesterday that I probably wouldn't feel
better for about ten weeks.

Two days ago I was feeling pretty good and
actually went downstairs to visit with some people who

332 | Audrey Sofield Barber

are temporarily staying downstairs. Their names are Arnie and Ruth. They are such nice people.

They are originally from Wellsboro but the winters scared them away and they moved to Florida but they come here every year for two or three weeks. We talked (or should I say, "I talked") for about an hour and that was my outing for the day. Whoopee!

Yesterday I went to the framer and I couldn't believe how wonderful the picture of Captain Sofield came out. It's the picture that will be hanging in the Court House courtroom of the Magistrate. When I saw it I started tearing up. Then when I got home and took a picture of the framed photo it shows a reflection of me looking up at it in a very ethereal way and I decided to keep it that way.

Still Under The Weather
July 14

I have been fighting the weakness that goes with this pneumonia, et cetera and it just doesn't seem to go away. Now there are only two weeks before the coming reunion and a wonderful visit from my daughter, Leslie, and my great-granddaughter, Kyra. In keeping with that thought, I received an email from Matt Herring, the main coordinator for the reunion, telling me that they were coming to Wellsboro to do some preparing for it and that they would try to stop by to see me. That gave me a boost and I got dressed for it at about 11AM, yesterday, and when they didn't come I got in the car and drove over to Woodland Park where some of the doins' are going to be held and they weren't there. Soon after that there was a huge rainstorm including thunder and lightning and so I went back home.

334 | Audrey Sofield Barber

I got back into my round-the-house-when-you're-sick robe and sat down to eat and the phone rang and guess who it was: yes, it was them, the re-enactors. They gave me a half an hour to finish eating and get redressed and then, the three of them came over.

Left to right: Bruce Petrol, Gerry Reigle, Matt Herring and me

There was Matt and a man that I hadn't met or corresponded with before, Garry Reigle, and sweet Bruce Petro, who plays Captain Sofield in all the re-enactments. Bruce calls me, "Miss Audrey." That's how they talked in the 1800s and I love it.

When they came up here I gave them all a big hug and we sat and talked for two hours. They told me that when they found out that my relatives were coming out they hired a horse drawn carriage so that Leslie, Kyra and I could ride in it to the procession that will go to the cemetery on the last day of reunion. I am anxious to get pictures of that ride. I am also always going to be mentally prepared for disappointment, though, because at my age you realize that not all plans work out the way they are supposed to (take most weddings, for instance).

While they were here, Garry had a very authentic looking Union Soldier hat. I learned that there were three types of hats. There was the Slouch, which the officers used to wear on certain occasions. There was the Kepi, which the officers also wore on different occasions, and then there was the Forage Hats that the lower ranking soldiers wore. That was the one that Garry had on. The reason it was called the Forage Hat was because it had a larger bonnet so that when they were traveling they could forage eggs, fruit or whatever food they could fit into the hat. Here is a picture of Bruce wearing the Slouch hat.

Just before they were about to leave, Matt said to me, "We brought you a little gift." He pulled a Bucktail out of his pocket and gave it to me. I don't know if you, who aren't doing what I am doing could know how appreciative and thrilled I was when he gave it to me, but I was elated! Any connection with my Wellsboro past is deeply appreciated. Those three men have no idea what happiness that little visit brought to me. I deeply appreciate that connection.

Update
July 21

Well, here it is July 21 and I'm still hobbling around like an eighty-one-year-old. Hobbling is not my usual thing: I usually prance. It seems that when the doctor said that my strength wouldn't return until ten weeks from June 26, she wasn't kidding. My good days are about every other day. Brian left for work today and will be gone for some time and it's a little lonely around here but I AM WOMAN, AND I'LL SURVIVE! Isn't that brave of me?

About six weeks ago when I still had my HP printer and it decided to retire, I still had one unopened black ink cartridge left over and I hated to throw it away so I took it to the office supply place here in Wellsboro called TOP (Tioga Office Products) over at 96 East Street. No that is not across the street from me—surprise, surprise—but rather four miles. I decided to take it over there and see if they could sell it at a discount and they could keep the money. When I went in I was greeted by a charismatic lady with long beautiful auburn hair named Darla DeBloise. I offered the black ink cartridge to her and she said that she would call me if and when it sold because she wanted me to have the money. Yes, that's right, this is, it seems, the Wellsboro way.

Darla DeBloise and me

I argued a little at first but went ahead and accepted her offer. After a time I kind of forgot about it but one day, in fact it was the day that I started feeling sick, she called me and told me that they had sold the ink cartridge for $15 and that I could come and pick up the money anytime. I was really taken aback that it actually happened. I know, $15 isn't a windfall, but the attitude is so apropos to this little community. It was just one more happy arrow to go in my quiver.

Meanwhile I got sicker and went to the hospital and back out and was trying to get enough strength to get in my car and go and pick up the money. That came about last week and when I walked in there, there was a man in front of me and Darla was welcoming him in and she gave him a sisterly hug. Cute, cute, cute. Then I said, "Where's my hug?" and she came over and hugged me, too. She's a breath of fresh air and a little sunshine mixed in with it. If you are in a low mood and go in there when she is there, you'll feel better in no time.

A New Feeling
July 24

I am going to share a new feeling—a foreboding—
with my readers this morning. This has been going on
from the time I got sick starting around June 26: I, for the
first time, feel like I am facing my mortality. I knew that it
would probably come sometime and I'm hoping that it is a
temporary feeling. I know, we all have to go sometime but
not while I have such joy to forsake at this time.

The sheer joy that I felt since moving here has
changed almost to a foreboding. Brian has been re-
transferred from New Jersey back to Blakeslee,
Pennsylvania, which is still over 200 miles from
Wellsboro. Now that he is gone I have too much time to
think about my age, my new sickness, what my life is
going to be like without you reader(s) to share my life
with. I have many wonderful friends but they have their
lives, their families and their work or businesses to keep

them occupied. In a way I hate to change the mood of my book from my previous joy to one that has the tendency of melancholy. After all, we all have our ups and downs, our utter joys and our bouts with doldrums, but this seems to be more than that. This is a new feeling, one that makes me not want to go to bed at night. The minute I lay my head down at night I start getting this feeling that I am not going to wake up in the morning. I have never in my life felt that way. It's so disappointing because I seem to have found a perfect setting for my twilight years insofar as I have been happier than I had ever been. I have found my happy place, good friends, making a decent amount of money and most of all good health, but when that last one takes a dive the other ones take a back seat.

When I read the obituaries in the newspaper I see that there are plenty of people losing their lives in my age bracket. I knew this all along but when you are sick daily it starts to jump out at you. When I write my feelings to my dear friend and editor, Bo, he writes back with such encouraging and uplifting words of encouragement and it gives me spurt of mood revamping for the time. I can't share my feelings with my daughters as they have their own problems and why would I want to pile more on them?

My days used to be filled with activities and plans. I would get up in the morning and my imagination would start flourishing with ideas for what I was going to share with you that day. When I would go to bed at night I would feel fulfilled by remembering the day and what a good time I had just taking a walk down these unblemished streets and their perfectly trimmed lawns, beautiful flowers, smiling faces as we pass; the utter joy was unsurpassed. I felt, "this is where I belonged." Now when I go to bed at night I feel my kidney hurting and realizing that I should go to the doctor and see what that is all about but then it hits me that in just a few days my daughter and great-granddaughter will be here for the Bucktail Reunion, for the big event that I have been waiting months for … it is now at my doorstep. I can't see a doctor now because what if they put me in the hospital while what I have been waiting for is here? So I start counting the days when the joy of my family being here and the excitement of the reunion is right around the corner and the "what ifs" start keeping me from falling asleep.

After I first got out of the hospital I noticed that my kidney was getting little pangs here and there. When I went to my follow-up appointment, I told my doctor about it but she didn't seem to take it too seriously, but now, the pangs have started to turn into more constants. My next appointment with her is three weeks away and I have to decide whether to wait or to go now.

Looking back at my life, I have enjoyed pretty much good health. My worst health, believe it or not was when I was in my 20s and early 30s. I had had pneumonia twice in my 20s and constant kidney infections. It was back in my 20s that it was discovered that I had Atrial Fibrillation but had no idea that it could be fatal. My doctor gave me some pills that I took for a while and then I quit. While in my 20s I had chicken pox and measles and in my 30s I had mumps. Guess I was slow growing up. When in my 70s I got breast cancer and had a mastectomy but that was about 6 years ago and it seems to be in remission. It was at that time that my Atrial

Fibrillation was re-discovered. I know that this doesn't sound like I have been healthy but all and all I have hung on to my youth pretty well…until now. I know the doctor told me that it would be about 2 ½ months before I got my strength back but it sure is a slow moving 2 ½ months.

As I look out the window I see that beautiful Green with its adorable fountain that carries the Wynkin, Blynkin and Nod statue surrounded by a beautiful flower garden and a wrought iron circular fence only to be flourished by many healthy trees, it makes me want to go out there and be a part of it but when I do I get out of breath and just keep an eye on the next bench that I can rest on. My little town has prepared for the likes of me to move here because all the way down Main Street there are benches to rest on clear down to the end of town. Each block has about three benches on it with a dedication to a person that has passed and has made his/her mark on this little burg. Poor Brian, he loves to take walks—about five per day—and when I go with him I slow him down so much that I feel guilty so I just would rather go alone at my own pace. It's really hard when you feel like a young person and your body resists.

Well I will go on with the day and see if the mood gets any better. I loved it when I was sharing my joy with you but I'm sorry you must take the bad with the good. By the time you (all) read this I hope that my mood and health has changed all the while hoping that I'll be here to enjoy your reviews, whether they are rave or negative.

It is now 6:05 PM and my day ended much better than it started. I received an email from the Wellsboro Gazette and they said that they had my booklets ready. Then I went to the mailbox and found my newspaper in it and there was my picture on the front page advertising the article that you read when you turn to the "Living" section. It was such a good and thorough article with a picture of me sitting next to my great-great-grandparent's headstone. As we are not really good photographers, the only bad thing about the picture is my purse sitting next to me unzipped. I called the lady that wrote the article and thanked her for such a wonderful write-up. Who knows, I may even sleep tonight with no negative thoughts.

Today, all and all, ended up pretty good, with no further editing to be done either to my little booklets nor the newspaper article *and* Brian will be here on Saturday, if not Monday next, for good. I purchased ten newspapers and have to get busy tomorrow at the post office and start sending them out to friends and family.

All and all this journey has brought so much happiness to me that I just can't let this temporary illness (I hope) bring me down. Life is good even when it's not so good. Does that make sense?

Just A Little Update
July 30

I guess it's been a short while since I last had a conversation with you readers so I will tell you how I bungled up my daily living since then. (They don't call me Lucy for nothing).

First, I have been very depressed because of all the things that you have read about in the last chapter I wrote. When you are so joyful, as I was, and suddenly it is interrupted by something not in your control, such as a health problem like I experienced starting on June 27 and lasting and lasting and lasting, the joy turns into crying jags—and mine did. It would seem that every other day I could take a walk and the next day feel like I was going to collapse thinking, "Ahh! At last I'm getting well!" Then you can barely walk across the room without having to sit down and have your heart start pounding. Then to make things worse, it kept getting closer to Bucktail Reunion time and having Leslie and Kyra here for a week starting on the 31st of July and knowing that I was going to have to put on a happy face. All this time I had been emailing and calling her on the phone telling her how happy I have been since being here and she finally gets to come out here and see a big cry baby that couldn't even take them for a walk as I had planned.

Last Saturday I decided to go and give Mahjong a try and play at least one game. As it turned out there was an uneven amount of people there to play, so I packed up and came home and cried. It's probably good that it happened because I was not feeling up to sitting there for any length of time anyway. Since being sick my eyelids always feel heavy like they want to go to sleep but when I lie down my thoughts start to take over and my fear that I won't wake up keeps me awake.

The week before when I played Mahjong I had gone to the post office first to mail all my friends and relatives the wonderful newspaper article that came out on the Gazette, complete with picture about my book and me. I walked across the street to Pops Culture where the Mahjong games were going strong, sat down to play and realized that I had left my glasses at the Post Office. Julian, the owner, had his daughter go across the street to retrieve them so I was able to play. I purchased a drink and played a game and got tired and decided that I would come home. Once I got here my phone was ringing and lo and behold I had left my drink AND my glasses there. I'm pretty much always that way but lately it's been a lot worse. I have two pairs of glasses and today I can't find either one of them. I wonder where I left them this time. These are not just Dollar Store glasses, but both of them are prescription.

Now the kicker…

Yesterday I made all these arrangements to go to the airport that was supposed to be (in my confused mind) today. Brian didn't want me driving there alone so I called Kasey (the book store Kasey) and reluctantly asked her if she could ride along with me the fifty miles to the Elmira, New York, airport and that it wouldn't take up more than three hours. She said that she was having a busy day but that she would find someone for me. She called everyone she knew, she went on Facebook, she probably did an APB and finally found someone's mother in the next town over to go with me. I so appreciated it. I called the person and we made arrangements for me to pick her mother up at a gas station that was situated just before the freeway onramp. Then I took a little walk and thought that I would call Leslie and tell her to bring a jacket, as it's been rather chilly here. We talked for about twenty minutes and just before we hung up I said, "Well, see you tomorrow" and she said, "tomorrow?" Well it seems that I was to pick her up Thursday and not Wednesday. Oh my Gosh!!!! Now I had to call Michelle (Kasey's contact) and tell her how stupid I was and that my husband would probably be home by then and I would 't need her mother to go with me.

Previously that same day I had gotten to feel so badly that I had gone to see the doctor and she quadrupled my heart pacing medicine and gave me a little something to take away the crying jags. I went home and took the new meds and felt better than I had in weeks. No more heart fluttering and no more crying.

Last night at 7:30 PM I decided to take a little walk and ended up going to the Penn Wells Hotel where

Kasey's uncle, David Cox, works at the admittance desk. I had been told by many people that he was a Wellsboro history buff. When I walked up to his counter and introduced myself he showed himself to be a very friendly and welcoming man. I really enjoyed myself. I also learned something that has given me more exciting insight on where my great-grandparents may have lived. I told him that I suspected that according to one of the deeds that I had pulled indicated that they had lived next door to the Presbyterian Church on Main Street. There is a picture in my favorite book, the one called *Wellsboro from 1880 to 1920* that shows a picture of that church in 1880 and you can see a two story white house next to it. I had shown that to Scott Gitchell and he agreed with me that it very well could have been that house. It had been the Manse for the Presbyterian Church for a time. Now back to Dave Cox—this part is unbelievable—but he was raised in that house with his grandparents and he knew that it had been built in the 1800s.

This jigsaw puzzle just keeps growing and growing. I keep getting the feeling that I am living back in that era. All the prominent names, some that are still here, have been connected through deeds and newspaper articles just keep popping up. Every town has names that are well known to the town's history. In Riverside, California, where I was born and raised, it was Tavalone. The Tavalones owned practically everything in town. There was the bowling alley, TavaLanes, Tava Real Estate and Tava this and Tava that. In Utah, it was, of course, Smith and Young. That's not hard to figure out. Well here in Wellsboro it's Bodine, Bache, Robinson, Niles, Packer and Seele, most of whom still have ancestors still living here. I may be leaving some of them out, but they are outstanding.

I have found in newspapers and deeds that my relatives had connections with all of them. I have a feeling, like I have said before, that my great-grandfather wanted to climb that ladder but maybe didn't live long enough to get to the top with his cohorts. I may be wrong but that's my take on him. His uncle, Joseph Sofield, I believe had more money and panache because he owned a lot of property around town and seemed to be taking care of the rest of the family at different times. There was one recorded paper that showed that my great-great-grandfather had filed for bankruptcy and it showed the different debtors that had to be paid. Most of them were small debts but there were many $100.00 loans from Joseph Sofield that would have to be satisfied from the bankruptcy.

You will pardon me but today's entry has been somewhat of a mishmash of thoughts and feelings but I'VE BEEN SICK!

The Reunion
July 31

I will start with the day that I went to pick up
Leslie and Kyra. That was on Thursday, July 31. I had
gone to the doctor and she increased my heart medication
so I was feeling better.

I knew that I had to have someone go with me to
the airport and I didn't have the nerve to ask the lady that
Kasey had arranged for me again so I asked Toni Smith
who owns the little store Natural Ways if she could spare
about three hours and go with me. I just don't know my
way around here if I step foot out of Wellsboro. Oh, I can
make it to Mansfield (12 miles) or Tioga (about another 12
miles in the other direction), but that's about it. So Toni
went with me and we made it just in time. They met me
out in front of the small terminal. On our way there Leslie
had texted me that they were taxiing in and that her plane
was one step above a crop duster. I hate those things.

The Greeting

We chatted all the way home and they got acquainted with Toni. Then when we pulled into Wellsboro we went to drop Toni off at her store and we all wanted to go in and see it. Here's what it looks like now. If you go to the left you get healthy and go to the right and you get pretty. Natural Ways deals in health products and Rue 2 has cute clothes. A real cozy little place.

To be healthy, go to the left, if you want to be pretty go to the right

From there we went to my apartment and they seemed to love it. When we got there Brian had just arrived from work.

There was a lot of catching up to do. Kyra, my great-granddaughter, being seventeen, had decided that she was going to make me eat right and get me healthy again and boy did she mean it. She hid the salt, insisted on throwing away all the food that she didn't think that I should eat. The next thing she did was to insist on going grocery shopping and buy healthy foods for me. She's a sweetheart but I HAVE TO HAVE MY SALT!

Now here's another Lucy thing that happened on the second day they were here. Kyra decided to clean out (and I mean "clean out" my refrigerator. After she got done, she came in and showed me a picture that she had taken with her phone. It was a picture of a box of cherries that I had in the fridge with something shiny on top. I couldn't figure out what the shiny thing was…until they told me that they had found my glasses. That brought on some laughs. Leslie said, "Mom, you never disappoint me."

August 1: The First Day of the Reunion

Not much was going to be going on with the reunion on the first day that we would get involved with as they were just going to be setting up tents, et cetera, over at a park…not The Green. The re-enactors would be camping out there and preparing for the next day's barbeque, so what a surprise it was when I looked across the street and saw the men in uniform having their pictures taken and being interviewed by the local web site called "wellsborohomepage.com." I told the girls that I was going down there and see who I could see. Here are the three good looking "soldiers" in their blue uniforms.

Don Nunamaker, Doug Foster and Matt Herring, all Civil War descendants

Later on that day I took the two girls, Leslie and Kyra, over to the courthouse where Leslie's great-great, and Kyra's four-time, great-grandfather had worked as Justice of the Peace.

Leslie and Kyra on the courthouse steps

We then took a little ride around the neighborhood to look at the beautiful Victorian houses and they were both going ooooh ahhhhh, "Oh look at that one, look at this one." They both loved it here.

Then later in the day I looked out the window and saw a group of the re-enactors heading for my house. All of us ran down there and we stood on the steps and talked for about two hours.

On my front porch

August 2, 2014

Today is the *Big Day*!!! This is the day that we would all be sitting on The Green presenting to the locals and the Wellsboro visitors our presentations of The Bucktails. There were books, a man that whittled little Union Soldiers, a man that had studied medicines that were used on the battlefields. Leslie and Kyra were really captivated by his presentation. Unfortunately I didn't get a chance to go and see them all because I was presenting my little teaser booklet.

Wellsboro Roots

By Audrey Sofield/Barber

After about three hours of this I was ready to take my nap. I've had to do this every afternoon since I have been sick and my sweet little Kyra, sat in for me and got many email addresses from people who wanted to know when the book would be ready to purchase.

Kyra gathering email addresses

All went very well. Then that evening at 6PM was to be the "Pig Barbeque." We were rested by then and off we went to the local Woodland Park where the re-enactors had it set up with tents that they had slept in the night before. They wanted it to look very much like the battlefield camps. The wives and children were wearing 1800s clothes. I am sure that a lot of hard work went into that. We were approached many times by other re-enactor descendants where they introduced themselves and told a little about their ancestors. They all knew who Captain Sofield was because he was the lead captain, always played by Bruce Petro. We were so proud! I am so glad that Leslie and Kyra got to experience this because this was their roots too.

At the barbeque

The kids

August 3: The Horse-Drawn Day

This was the big day that we were so looking
forward to: the day that I'd get to ride in a horse drawn
carriage up Main Street and wave to all the onlookers.
That was to be my fifteen minutes (or less) of fame. We
would be going up to the cemetery to hear a eulogy given
by Matt Herring for the Wellsboro Soldiers who had been
killed and buried here. We were so anxious…but Mother
Nature had other ideas. I had often wondered why The
Green didn't have an automatic sprinkling system, nor
does the house that I live in and it has a great lawn…now
I know why! Heavens little sprinkling system was on time
on August 3, 2014, because after we all arose and got all
dressed up and ready to head down to the front of the
house with a carrot in our hands (to give to the horse) I

happened to look outside and it was literally pouring down rain!!! About that time my phone rang and our little parade had been called off. It was Matt, giving us the disappointing news. I could tell that he hated to do it but he said that it just wouldn't be practical…to which I agreed. Instead we all went out to eat at Nelle's fancy upscale Sunday Buffet, The Lambs Creek Food and Spirits in Mansfield. We really had a nice and fun time at the Buffet, but not quite as much fun as it would have been in the horse drawn carriage.

At the buffet

We all were so grateful for the wonderful thought that Matt and Bruce came up with regarding the horse and buggy idea and we'll forever be heartened by that act of kindness. (And they're not even from Wellsboro!!)

This reunion will be in our memories for the rest of our lives and we are so humbled by the attention that was paid to us, as Captain Sofield's ancestors.

I hope that we can all keep in touch, through Facebook if nothing else. My whole book was leading up to this reunion and it was well worth the wait!

The End
August 11

Well here it is: the end of my quest—or at least writing about it. I hate for this book to end, as it has been such good company to me by connecting with all of you. I am trying to think of an interesting sequel to this book because I know that by my just being here in Wellsboro things of interest will come up and I won't have you to share them with. As I think back there are things that I have left out of this book that should have been added...like my husband's picture.

Then a very important lady that came with Brian on Saturday and stayed until Monday, Mary Simmons. She works with Brian and is one of the sweetest ladies that I have ever met. She enjoyed herself here even though she had never heard of Bucktails and said that she got quite an

This is Brian

education just by seeing the reunion. She was a delight as a houseguest.

On Saturday, August 2, on the second day of the reunion, while taking email addresses and handing out my booklets, there were other authors selling their completed books.

At a table behind me I kept hearing a man say "Captain Sofield" while he would be endeavoring to sell his book. I would turn around to see who was saying it and I never could figure it out. Well, Leslie did figure it out so she went to him, "him" being Bill Robertson who was selling his book called *The Bucktail, Brothers of the Fighting 149th*. Leslie bought the book for me and I truly love it. I recommend it for anyone wanting to read about little personal things that these "boys" went through while marching off to war. He has some fictional characters in it along with some real people, two of them that caught my eye being, Captain Sofield, because he was the lead captain of Company A, and another being Sergeant Warriner. Sergeant Warriner is the great-grandfather of Tom Warriner who still lives here in Wellsboro. I have been trying to get together with him since I first moved here back in January so that I could have my picture taken with us together and now I did it and here it is.

According to Tom Warriner, his relative is Benjamin A. Warriner…then later in the list is an Ira Warriner and he figures that he is a relative of his, too.

Part Three: Summation

Summation

As I look back on this wonderful decision that I made less than one year ago, and that was~~~to come to Wellsboro and write this book, I try to think of what I have not only accomplished but what I have come to discover. As I had said in one of the chapters, I have lived in many towns and in six states: California, Utah, Texas, Wyoming, Hawaii, and now, Pennsylvania.

I feel that what is missing from those places is this: here, where I live, is close to town…you can walk to a friend's house, a play, a restaurant, shopping for anything because everything is so close and I guess that gives the people who live here that community feeling that so many people crave. When walking down the street here I don't think that I ever go without someone saying, "Hi Audrey" and I've only been here 7 ½ months.

I recently read an article I found in Google.com that came from the New York Times titled, "A Quaint

Little Town with Quiet Things To Do." The opening sentence says this: *"A long row of tall, black gaslights, standing as ramrod straight as soldiers on a parade ground, stretches for several blocks down the middle of Main Street in Wellsboro, PA. They cast a gauzy, cozy, stay-a-while glow."*

It goes on to say that you can set your watch back fifty years. It set my mind to wondering what made it that way. I guess that it's because it hasn't been damaged by the suburban sprawl where people don't know their neighbors and the sense of community has been lost. We don't have the malls that take business away from our beloved store owners. This place hasn't been transformed but has kept the old "tyme" spirit. It is basically isolated from large towns and is steeped in history that reaches clear back to the Civil War.

Last night Brian and I went out to dinner at the Penn Wells hotel/restaurant and as I approached the lobby, the man behind the counter, Dave Cox, said, "Well, if it isn't Audrey Sofield Barber. Then when we went in to eat, the man in the table behind us said, "Is that Audrey Sofield Barber?" I turned around and saw Don Nunamaker, one of the Bucktail Re-enactors with his wife, Sylvia. They were from a town called St. Mary, Pennsylvania. His wife was saying how she had only been here twice but loved the feeling she gets when she is here...my point being, it isn't just me: everyone says it.

Now the top priority on my list of what I have accomplished by my being here is that I brought back the Sofield name. When my great-grandmother and her boys left here in 1878 or 1879 there didn't remain one Sofield ancestor here, but I have put it back where it belongs. I

now have my great-grandfather's picture hanging in the
courtroom in the court house and that makes me feel so
good. Being eighty-one years old I know that I am not
going to be here much longer and there is no progeny to
take my place here, but now the people in this town, at
least the ones who go to court, will see that picture and
know that a proud man gave up a good career to go off
and fight for what he believed in and actually died for it,
and that he used to sit with a gavel in his hand, marry
people, buy property and took an active part in this
wonderful little town. I wish that there could be a street or
a landmark named after him like Bache, Norris and others
that played a big part here back then but I, at least, got a
picture hung up.

Another big accomplishment that gives me such
satisfaction is that my two daughters, Randa and Leslie
and my great-granddaughter, Kyra Stewart, also got to
come here and see where some of their roots were. I so
wish that my other daughter, Debi, could come here but
right now that is on hold. My son, Anthony (Pepe) lives
on Maui and I don't expect him anytime soon, and my
other son, David, lives in California and, like everyone, has
to work and I don't look out the window expecting to see
him drive up either, but at least three of the little Sofield
sprigs got to be here and enjoy it.

Last, but certainly not least, I had the privilege of
meeting and enjoying the company of those wonderful re-
enactors. They are such a respectful and encouraging
group of men and so are their beautiful wives and
children. It's truly been a fulfilling time!

So all in all, *Mission Accomplished!* From searching
my history, making friends, loving the little town, getting a

perfect apartment overlooking The Green, to making a name for my ancestors. All has ended well!

ABOUT THE AUTHOR

Audrey Lynne Sofield Sanchez Barber was born in Riverside, California, on March 2, 1933, an only child. Her parents lived on Marlborough Street in the northern part of Riverside at that time. Her parents were Alfred Jay Sofield and Frances Byrd Handler Wartell Sofield (she always changed Byrd to Bernice on important papers as she hated the name Byrd). *There was a brief and secret marriage to a Marc Wartell that she is still seeking.

On October 9, 1948, her mother passed away from cancer when Audrey was fifteen years old. She was left to live alone with her poor Dad. He didn't know how to raise a teen-ager but he did his best. (Is there even a way?) Audrey didn't handle being a teenager very well and was somewhat rebellious. On October 28, 1948, she met her husband to be, Carmelo (Chito) Sanchez and three years later was married to him (she wants to write another book about how that came about) on December 22, 1951. He had joined the Navy and was on a trip to Korea on the USS Manchester CL-83, a light cruiser, about one week and a half after they were married. Nine months later in San Francisco, California, at Oak-Knoll Naval Hospital, where his ship was docked, on September 13, 1952, their first-born daughter, Debra Lynne, arrived after he had come back from overseas. Then he went back overseas again, leaving Audrey pregnant with their second daughter, Randa Rae. He was still overseas when she was born in Norco Naval Hospital, in Norco, California, on May 21, 1954. He came back again and was getting toward the end of his enlistment period of four years, he went overseas one more time, this time for only five months instead of the usual seven months. He went on the Ernest G. Small DD-214, which was a destroyer escort. After coming back, this time, he had served his four years and again was a civilian. Their next daughter, Leslie Noel Sanchez was born on December 22, 1955, in Loma Linda Hospital, Loma Linda, California.

Over time Chito became an electrician they purchased their first home at 5527 Babb Avenue in Arlington, California, in 1956.

On October 3, 1962, they had their first son, Anthony Pepe Sanchez and then the last child born, also a son, was David William Sanchez. He was born on March 3, 1964. Both the boys were born in Riverside, California. In 1974 after all three of the daughters were married and two of them had moved far away, they followed Leslie and her husband Steve Stewart to Nevada City, California, and in Nevada County which was about 500 miles away from

Riverside. Then they worked their way down to Meadow Vista, California, in Placer County. Their sons, Pepe and David, were ten and twelve respectively. They had purchased a very small home and that episode is worth another memoir.

In 1977 she attained her real estate license and began working as a real estate agent in Auburn, California, just a stone's throw from Meadow Vista. She had worked for three companies: Bertrando & Associates, Allstate Realtors and Hometown Real Estate.

In 1979 they purchased an acre in Meadow Vista at 17541 Vista Court and built a beautiful 3000 square foot home overlooking Lake Combie. Then in 1981 she walked out of their beautiful home and left, to try her life as a single person. She left her two boys, aged seventeen and eighteen at home and got a housemate and started living with her in Auburn while still trying to make a living in real estate. 1981 was not a good year to make a living in that business, as she found out.

In September of 1982 she met and fell hard for Brian Barber who had owned his own real estate company across town from her in Newcastle. Later that year she obtained a divorce from Chito. This was at a very vulnerable time financially for all three of them but Brian and Audrey took a chance on each other and got married in Reno, Nevada, on September 27, 1985 and moved to Hawaii thereafter.

Now in 2014 she is still married to the same man and that has been a merry-go-round to which she plans to write about in another memoir, if time allows. After all she is eighty-one.

For a time, while writing this book, she is residing in Wellsboro, Pennsylvania, and feels a magnetic pull for this place because of her "Roots" here. Time will tell whether she stays here, dies here or leaves and goes back to Hawaii where her husband Brian wants to live again.

Stay Tuned!

Made in the USA
Middletown, DE
11 July 2022

69048045R00215